CRITICAL REVIEWS

I have known Juhani Wahlsten for many years. I met him in Turku, Finland while I was working with the Swedish National Hockey Team in 1996. We discussed his work and research done to aid amateur hockey coaches all over the world. I took some of his work home with me to Detroit, Michigan. I shared his research with other Youth Hockey Coaches. Everyone I showed his work to was impressed. Th   n reasons I enjoyed Juhani's on-ice teaching methodology were twofold:

1. Players involvement – many players doing similar s⌐
2. Players were executing fundamental skills   ⌐erent speeds.

With the cost of ice rentals constantly going up,   ⌐nce amateur hockey organizations have to give each player an o⌐   ⌐mprove is – to put more than one team on an ice surface and divide th⌐   ⌐ halves – length or width wise or thirds, using each zone as Juhani has advocated. Juhani's dedication to this project of improving hockey players' skills through proper practice organization is the best chance to raise a player's level of skills and play. I recommend adding this excellent book to your hockey library.

Barry Smith,
Detroit Red Wings Associate Coach

I have known Juuso (Juhani) as an international hockey developer for over 15 years. During the last six years we have worked together in developing young hockey players in Turku, Finland. During this time I have also come to know and work with Tom Molloy in the development of international hockey. "Even though hockey is a Canadian game, it has developed to the current stage through international interaction between different hockey cultures. These cultures meet at their best at the professional leagues. Juuso's and Tom's book – *Hockey Coaching: The ABCs of International Hockey* starts a new era of hockey development at its grass-root level. *The ABCs of International Hockey* data base is not only a series of different drills and exercises, it is a system that sets the standards for player development based on experience, know-how and competence. It can be used wherever the game is played. This system is also a communication tool between different hockey cultures that allows the know-how of the world's best hockey developers to be available to amateur coaches in an understandable and workable form. Both the coaches and the players learn by doing.

Vladimir Yursinov, assistant coach of Russian National Team
1974-1992, Head Coach of 1998 silver medal winning Russian
Olympic Team in Nagano Olympic Games, TPS Turku, Finland
Coach 1992-1998: developer of 40 NHL players in his coaching
career, 18 during his work in Turku, Finland.

During two years of Juuso's coaching I experienced that his theme "Enjoy the Game" is not just words; but with Juuso it becomes action on ice – a way to learn the game and enjoy it. No matter what level one reaches in his hockey career I believe that coaches are in key positions in young peoples' lives. I highly recommend this book to coaches.

> *Saku Koivu, Captain of the Finnish National Team in Nagano Olympics, Montreal Canadiens star player, ex-student of Juhani Wahlsten's hockey class at the Aurajoki Sports High School in Turku, Finland.*

"Ice hockey is a GAME on ice, not a WAR on ice". It is a SKILL sport, especially at an early age. When the players have learned the ABCs and start to understand the main principles of the game, then . . . but only then . . hockey will be more like a combat over all the ice. "It is not enough sweating during a game; you must show skill, too . . ." wrote Anatoli Tarasov many years ago. This fundamental book is a handbook for the enthusiastic, but inexperienced coach/instructor. There is only ONE HOCKEY, but you can interpret and develop the hockey you want.

> *Verner Persson, Internationally recognized player developer, AIK Stockholm, Sweden, named Hockey Leader of the Year, 1997-98, by Swedish Hockey journalists.*

"I've attended many clinics and practices with Tom Molloy. During Tom's practices you learn to play hockey and you also have a lot of fun."

> *Dany Heatley, MVP Air Canada Cup, Calgary Buffaloes, Midget AAA, 1998*

In Search of the Best Hockey for Young People

Enjoy the Game

Juhani Wahlsten
Tom Molloy

Hockey Coaching:

The ABCs of International Hockey

In search of the best hockey for young people.

Levels 0-2   **Book 1**

**Basic Manual for All Coaches
Cards for Beginners to Age 9**

IEMS

ΣHA

European Hockey Academy

PRODUCTIONS

Hockey Coaching: The ABCs of International Hockey

by
Juhani Wahlsten and Tom Molloy

First Printing – September 1998

Copyright © 1997 by Juhani Wahlsten and Tom Molloy

Canadian Cataloguing in Publication Data

Wahlsten, Juhani.
     Hockey coaching: the ABCs of international hockey
     ISBN 1-894022-10-6

1. Hockey – Coaching.   I. Molloy, Tom, 1947-

II. International Educational Management Systems.

III. Title.

GV848.25.W34 1998   796.962'007   C98-920186-4

Hockey Cards Designed By:
Hemmo Karhu, H & P, Finland
Jan-Erik Nylund, Typopress, Finland
Finnish Ice Hockey Association
European Hockey Academy © IEMS

Cover Design:
Brian Danchuk, Brian Danchuk Design, Regina, Saskatchewan

Designed, Printed and Produced in Canada by

Centax Books, a Division of PrintWest
Publishing Director – Margo Embury
1150 Eighth Avenue, Regina, Saskatchewan, Canada S4R 1C9
(306) 525-2304   Fax: (306) 757-2439

ACKNOWLEDGEMENTS

We would like to acknowledge the many hockey coaches who have directly or by association contributed to the ideas in this book and Marian Moser and Jim Regan who have helped by proofreading the manual.

We want to thank and acknowledge the people we have played with, coached teams or camps with or whose clinics we have attended: Terry Johnson, Willie Desjardins, Mike Johnston, Tim Bothwell, Verner Persson, Slava Lener, Bob Toner, Scott MacDonald, Murray Heatley, Wally Kozak, Armand Belcourt, Curtis Brackenbury, John M. Cleveland, Court Dunn, Mike Berridge, Doug Cronk, Stewart Behie, Vladimir Yursinov, George Hill, Randy Murray, George Kingston, Bob Murdoch, Hans Lindberg, Ludak Bukac, Kjell Larsen, Dave King, Roger Nielson, Juhani Tamminen, Jukka Koivu, Harri Jalava, Jouko Lukkarila, Jani Mesikämmen, Robert Beale and Horst Wein.

We would like to acknowledge and thank Gaston Schaeffer for his contributions to the skating progressions.

I want to thank all my first coaches who taught me to enjoy the game in my home town Kuopio, Finland, and all of the other players and colleagues whose names are not mentioned, but who have worked with us to produce the system.

A special thanks to professor Osmo Kivinen and his research group at the Research Unit for the Sosiology of Education at University of Turku, and to Leena Jääskeläinen, the principal of Santa Claus Sports Institute, at Rovaniemi; Jani Mesikämmen, who has assisted in keeping the material in order; last but not least, Gill and Peter Allison, my great English teachers.

We especially want to thank our wives, Leena Wahlsten and Cathy Molloy, and our children, Sami and Jali Wahlsten and Colleen, Annie, Melissa and Jim Molloy for their patience while we have worked on this book.

Juhani Wahlsten and Tom Molloy

THE AUTHORS

Developing individual skills and using them in game situations; better use of the ice; combining the best of European and North American hockey strategies and training, Juhani Wahlsten and Tom Molloy have created a teaching and learning system to make practices both productive and fun.

A hockey coach and educator, Wahlsten played for the Finnish National Team for eleven years, participating in three Olympic Games and five World Championships. Captain of the team for many years, he was named to the Finnish Ice Hockey Hall of Fame. In charge of International Coaching Development for the Finnish Ice Hockey Association, Wahlsten has had a successful coaching career at the professional level in Finland, Germany and Switzerland, and at the international level with the Finnish Under-20 National Team. He was the first European coach to be offered a coaching position in the NHL, by Scotty Bowman, then of the Buffalo Sabres. Wahlsten's vision for international sports cooperation and communication has resulted in his involvement in international exchanges, symposiums and the production of books and video material.

Co-author Tom Molloy, also a hockey coach and educator, played in the United States Hockey League before returning to Calgary to teach and coach. He is certified at the Advanced Level 1 and has instructed up to the intermediate level for the CHA. Molloy has coached hockey at almost all levels, including assistant coach at the University of Calgary. As a guest coach or head instructor, he has used this teaching system with great success in Canada, Korea, Norway, United States, Finland and Austria. The system has also been introduced in France and Turkey. He has also participated in numerous international presentations with Juhani Wahlsten and Vladimir Yursinov, the 1998 Silver Medal Russian Olympic coach.

Learn by doing and **Enjoy the Game**, these principles are key to the *ABCs of International Ice Hockey*. The practices inspired by these teaching principles will help to develop skilled players, great teamwork, creative and exciting hockey.

TABLE OF CONTENTS

FOREWORD

The Finnish Ice Hockey Association reorganized its coach training system and the contents of the training in 1991. The game of ice hockey is seen now more than it used to be as a combination of several components. This is reflected in hockey practice as well. At the same time the natural everyday exercise of children has decreased and organized coach-led practices have increased. The practice sessions of younger juniors requires them to develop not only their technical, but also their playing skills against the opponents, and (at the same time) their thinking-hockey sense. The task of a coach is also to utilize limited ice time more effectively and involve as many players as possible in quality action on ice.

Hockey Coaching: The ABCs of International Ice Hockey is an answer to these and many other requirements of modern hockey practice. It is the task of a coach to transmit the hockey know-how of earlier generations to new generations. In *Hockey Coaching: The ABCs of International Ice Hockey* one can see Juhani Wahlsten's long hockey and life experience. He has transferred part of his own experience into hockey practices. Practices are not just practices. They must also include valuable know-how about how different qualities are successfully developed and how to use the ice effectively. Players learn by doing and coaches strengthen the learning process with their guidance. These practices also make up a program by which a coach can progress as the skill level advances. They also help the players to understand the game and its requirements better.

Hockey Coaching: The ABC´s of International Ice Hockey supports the contents of the coach training of the Finnish Ice hockey Association and is an excellent help to all coaches in carrying out hockey practices.

Erkka Westerlund
Director of Development
Finnish Ice Hockey Association

PART I

•

EFFICIENT USE OF THE RINK

The ABCs
of International Ice Hockey

The ABCs of International Ice Hockey includes all possible aspects of development and self-improvement. It is focused on the game itself. There are numerous modified games to create movement and understanding of game principles. Gamelike activities also promote fitness and make practices a lot of fun. It is a "learn by doing" method.

Anyone who joins a hockey team wants to PLAY hockey. This is why players always organize their own street and ice-hockey games when there is no coach around.

Our idea is to promote the game by following the natural way that a player would learn the game with his friends. We give coaching guidelines to help the coach and players **learn by doing**. Everything takes time. The coach has to repeat the exercises many times to develop effective players and become an effective organizer. Therefore we use very few take off points in our on-ice practices. The repetition, with little instruction and maximum movement during practice, is the key to learning.

The Four Playing Roles are the theme that we follow throughout the entire teaching system, in both the skills and the games.

1. **The first playing role develops individual offensive skills, using drills and games.**

2. **The second playing role practices supporting the puckcarrier by getting open, screening, picking and giving width and depth to the offense.**

3. **The third playing role focuses on individual defensive skill, learning to play a defensive one-on-one, always maintaining the defensive side.**

4. **The fourth playing role is concerned with supporting the first checker by covering man to man or in a zone.**

Another consideration is the loose puck situation or transitions from defense to offense. The drills progress to going on defense after losing the puck, and going on offense after regaining puck possession. These games have natural transition situations which are hard to duplicate using drills.

We try to use common sense. When the great athletes of another era learned to play by scrimmaging for hours they were not wasting time. The NBA gets its great basketball players from the big city playgrounds, where the kids play pick up games all day and learn to create moves that most coaches would never allow. In the last 20 years we have become focused on teaching drills instead of hockey, making practice very static and not very enjoyable.

Playing games in practice doesn't mean that the time is wasted. However, every simplified and modified game in our system has a purpose. The drills are important in developing individual skills. These skills are improved when modified games are played. Once the physical skills are developed the players must learn to use them in realistic gamelike situations where they are forced to read the play and make good decisions.

Anatoli Tarasov revolutionized on-ice practices and worked to develop the complete athlete in ice hockey. Our system is a synthesis of all the techniques used in the international game. The drills and games are not the answer; they are techniques for a systematic way of repeating the concepts that teach a player **to be in the right place at the right time.** The system deals with both on- and off-ice practices. A good on-ice practice is best because the ice is where the game is played.

QUALITY PRACTICE

Ice hockey was first learned very naturally. It was based on the players own initiative and creativity. The natural way was learning by doing. Times have changed and now players learn the game in drill-oriented practices organized by the coaches. And so we ask: "What is the most effective yet natural way to learn to play the game during organized practices?"

To start with, hockey is learned by moving. To guarantee hockey movements the coach must be a very good organizer. He must learn how to use the ice effectively and avoid "dead moments" when the players are standing in line, doing nothing for long periods of time.

This teaching method is designed to help the coach run effective and active practices. It contains 18 different formations from which the coach can operate and manage. He only needs to handle the lines or rows of players which are positioned in various parts of the rink. The advantage of minimizing drill formations and repeating familiar take off positions is unquestionable. The players and coach become very familiar with the basic formations, leaving more time for practicing hockey. This simple organization allows the coach to manage effective practices. This enhances his coaching ability and self-esteem.

The most challenging part of our 25 years of coaching experience has been to find the simplest patterns for practice organization. From these simple basic formations you can work on all hockey skills and tactics.

We have coded the formations and exercises in a progressive manner, from simple to more difficult. The coach should choose the formations and individual or team tasks that suit his practice goals, with his players skill development and age in mind. This system can be used from the beginner to the professional level.

We have given the formations and some examples of drills and exercises that can be done. The coach can expand on these basics by using the formations and his imagination and creativity. Add tasks, move pucks, have the players do coach-designated tasks at one end and read and react at the other; this is the art of coaching. We have included an exercise bank of drills as an extension of this system. The key idea is to create realistic situations, where they occur in a game.

The players are the ones that need to learn to play the game, developing the skills and using them at the right time and place. When the coach has his team practice skills in game-like situations the players will learn to play in all parts of the ice and also have the ability to read the play and react in imaginative and effective ways.

This system is natural because it duplicates realistic situations. Stay within the teaching system and add your own variations to the exercises and you will take a short cut to being a great coach.

BASIC FORMATIONS

A Learning to Balance and Move on the Ice

- skating posture
- beginning skating routines
- balance exercises on the ice
- power skating
- using the stick while skating

B Introduction To Basic Hockey Skills

- beginning goaltending
- goaltending stance
- goaltender movement
- playing various shots
- introduction to shooting
- passing and pass receiving
- gaining possession of loose pucks
- methods of angling and stickchecking the puckcarrier
- bodychecking techniques
- fakes with the puck
- angling the puckcarrier
- one-on-one contests

C Game Situation Skills

- movement with the puck
- one-on-one and all other situations that occur in a game
- cooperation of two players in various offensive and defensive situations
- cooperation of three, four and five players in offensive and defensive situations
- breakout plays
- power plays
- penalty killing

D Games and Modified Games

- regular game
- modified games with special rules often using only part of the rink
- games that emphasize specific player roles
- games that stress creating or restricting time and space
- games to teach team play
- special games for power play and penalty killing

E Cool Down Activities

- breakaway contests
- skill contests
- games for fun

F Goaltending Techniques

Goaltending teaching sequence, can be added to any module or during times when the goalie is inactive

BASIC FORMATIONS

A

A1

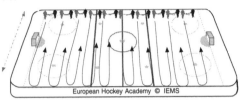

A2

A3

B

B1

B2

B

B3

B4

B5

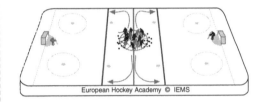

B6

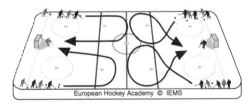

B7

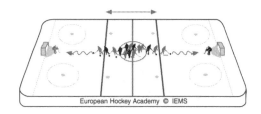

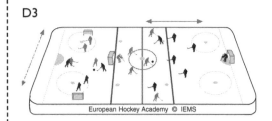

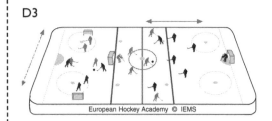

BASIC FORMATIONS

C

C1

C2

C3

D

D1

D2

D

D3

D4

E
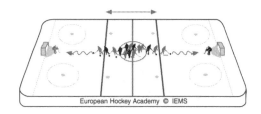

G

European Hockey Academy © IEMS

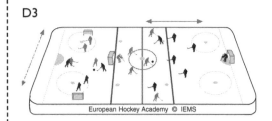

BASIC FORMATIONS – THE FIVE COMPONENTS OF A QUALITY ICE-HOCKEY PRACTICE

① A.   WARM-UP – Skating and Balancing

- skating posture
- beginning skating routines
- balance exercises on the ice
- power skating
- using the stick while skating

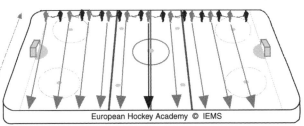

European Hockey Academy © IEMS

BASIC FORMATION A1

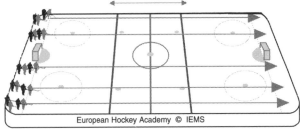

European Hockey Academy © IEMS

BASIC FORMATION A2

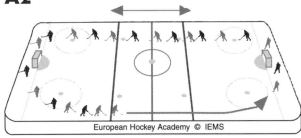

European Hockey Academy © IEMS

BASIC FORMATION A3

In **A** formation exercises, the coach instructs the players to line up in rows along the side boards or at the end of the rink. Beginners use **A** exercises to work on their skating posture. These exercises teach strength, balance and use of the skate blade edges. When the player can do all of the **A** exercises he or she will have a good comfortable skating posture. This posture is the essential building block and is the developmental base of all hockey skills.

A exercises progress to practicing puck handling in the essential balance position.

2 B.   WARM-UP – Basic Hockey Skills

- beginning goaltending
- goaltending stance
- goaltender movement
- playing various shots
- introduction to shooting
- passing and pass receiving
- gaining possession of loose pucks

- methods of stickchecking the puckcarrier
- bodychecking techniques
- fakes with the puck
- angling the puckcarrier
- one-on-one situations

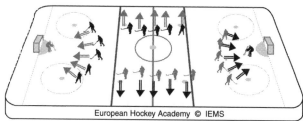

BASIC FORMATION B1

BASIC FORMATION B2

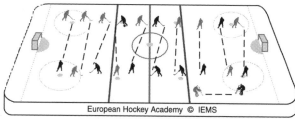

BASIC FORMATION B3

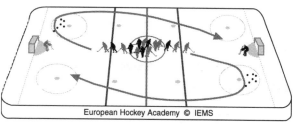

BASIC FORMATION B4

Individual Offensive and Individual Defensive Skills

The following skills are learned and practiced using **B** exercises; shooting, passing and pass receiving, as well as the basics of goaltending: stance, goalie movement and positioning. One-on-one skills of checking, winning loose pucks, faceoffs and stickhandling against an opponent are also practiced here.

The goaltender warm-up is a combination of **A** and **B** exercises that give the coach the chance to teach and practice different basic hockey skills. Later the players and goaltenders finish the **B** exercises with shooting routines.

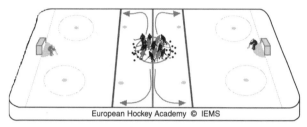

European Hockey Academy © IEMS

BASIC FORMATION B5

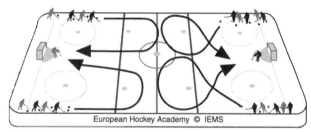

European Hockey Academy © IEMS

BASIC FORMATION B6

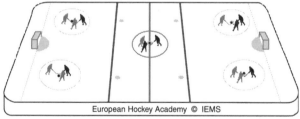

European Hockey Academy © IEMS

BASIC FORMATION B7

Handling the puck without looking at the puck is a prerequisite for learning offensive teamwork based on passing and pass receiving.

C. MAIN PART - Game Situation Skills

- movement with the puck
- all even-man and odd-man situations that happen in a game
- cooperation of two players in various offensive and defensive situations

- cooperation of three, four and five players in offensive and defensive situations
- breakout plays
- power plays
- penalty killing

European Hockey Academy © IEMS

BASIC FORMATION C1

European Hockey Academy © IEMS

BASIC FORMATION C2

European Hockey Academy © IEMS

BASIC FORMATION C3

EXERCISES - Game Situation

These drills are designed to be as gamelike as possible and skills are practiced in the areas on the ice where they occur in real games. For example, passing, receiving, breakouts, even-man and odd-man situations are all designed so they imitate games as closely as possible. By doing this the player learns to read the play and react in effective ways to situations. Timing routines and set breakout routines are also used to practice the options with which players are faced during games.

At the higher levels of skill the **C** drills are used more and the **A** and **B** drills are used only for review and for warm up.

4 D. GAMES – Individual and Team Skills

- regular game
- modified games with special rules often using only part of the rink
- games that emphasize specific player roles.

- games that stress creating or restricting time and space
- games to teach team play
- special games for power play and penalty killing

BASIC FORMATION D1

BASIC FORMATION D2

BASIC FORMATION D3

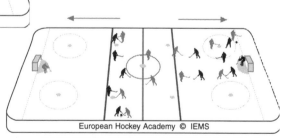

BASIC FORMATION D4

EXERCISES – Games and Modified Games

The **A**, **B** and **C** exercises only make sense if they help the players perform better during games. The games component is the most important section in the teaching system. Well-organized and meaningful games are the most realistic type of drill and, if the coach plans well, all of the basic skills and techniques can be practiced within games. The players enjoy playing games, so the enthusiasm for the practice is really improved. All even-man odd-man situations, including power plays, five-on-five, penalty killing and face-offs, are part of the **D** exercise routines.

⑤ E. COOL-DOWN ACTIVITIES

- breakaway contests
- skill contests

- games for fun
- races

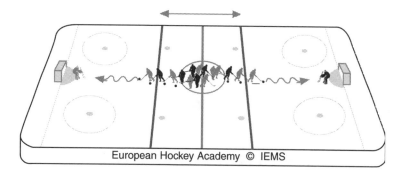

European Hockey Academy © IEMS

BASIC FORMATION E1

EXERCISES - Cool Down

Depending on how the coach designed the practice, the goalie may need to be either warmed up again or else be cooled down. In this system we have limited **E** drills to breakaway and penalty shot drills and races. As a basic routine it gives both the goalies and skaters work on scoring chances, and the players and coaches can have a lot of fun at the same time.

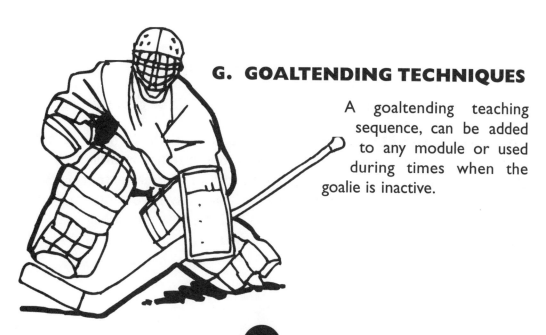

G. GOALTENDING TECHNIQUES

A goaltending teaching sequence, can be added to any module or used during times when the goalie is inactive.

DESCRIPTION OF THE ON-ICE PRACTICE FORMATIONS

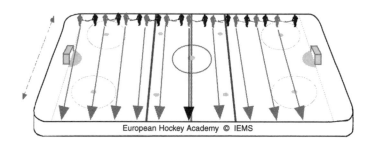

European Hockey Academy © IEMS

A1 BASIC FORMATION

The players are lined up along the side boards. The exercises are done with two groups or more.

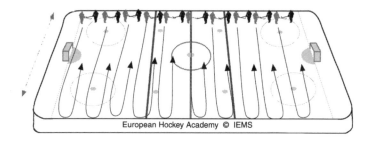

European Hockey Academy © IEMS

A100 VARIATION

For A100, in **A1** formation, players can return to the original starting points.

Teaching Points: A1 is the the most basic of all the formations. It is used first in the teaching system, because the skating distance is short. Divide the players into small groups, according to the colors of their jerseys or helmets, linemates, or simply number the players, so that they have room to maneuver without colliding with another player. When the first group has reached the opposite boards, then the next group leaves. Repeat the same drills in the opposite direction.

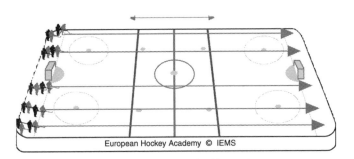

European Hockey Academy © IEMS

A2 BASIC FORMATION

The players are lined up at one end of the rink and divided into four groups. This allows the players to recover their energy between skating exercises. It also makes it easier for the instructor to watch the players. Most of the exercises and tasks are done between the blue lines.

Teaching Points: It is very important to use four or more groups in order to correct possible mistakes. It is also very important from the players' point of view, because to perform well the players need time to recover. Have the first group go and, when they cross the red line send the next group. When all groups are finished, then start from the other end of the rink. For older, more advanced players, have six or eight groups when working on speed development, in order to guarantee recovery between exercises.

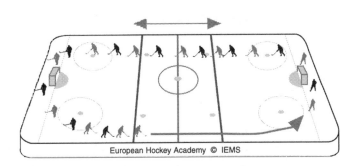

European Hockey Academy © IEMS

A3 BASIC FORMATION

The players skate around the ice. Various exercises can be done between the lines or around the ends.

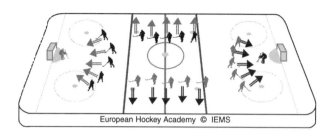

European Hockey Academy © IEMS

B1 BASIC FORMATION

This is the basic formation used in teaching shooting techniques. The players have pucks and line up within shooting distance from the board and the nets. The players will shoot either at the boards or the net.

Teaching Points: Practice a particular type of shot for a certain number of repetitions, e.g., "practice 50 shots." The instructors should skate around so they can watch each player shoot and either help him or tell him that he is shooting properly. This is also a good time to watch the goalies' basic stance and positioning.

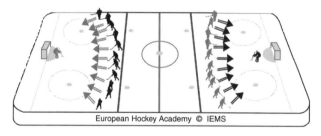

European Hockey Academy © IEMS

B2 BASIC FORMATION

Players line up with pucks inside the blue lines. The distance from the net is determined by the age of the players and the type of shot being used, the harder the shot the farther from the net.

Teaching Points: It is easiest to start the shots from the left of the goalkeeper. Halfway through the exercise the shots should start from the right. You can have players alternate from one side to the other, i.e., every second player shoot, skate in and shoot etc. Keep the shots below knee level and on the net. Players should focus on the netting behind the goalie and not on the goalie. Watch the goaltender to see if he centers himself with the puck and if he plays his angles properly. The next player doesn't shoot until the goalkeeper has completed his save. If the players miss the net they must do some exercise such as push-ups, sit-ups etc. This helps them concentrate and makes the practice more fun.

Examples of Variations of Basic Formation B2

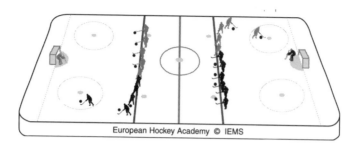

European Hockey Academy © IEMS

B 200 VARIATION

The basic **B2** formation with the players in a row at the blue line. Each player skates around the instructor or a pylon, takes a shot on net and follows her shot for a rebound. This exercise helps the goalie in playing angles.

Teaching Points: When cutting in, the player should protect the puck with his body, shielding it with an arm or leg. Move the pylon or coach in order to practice cutting in at various angles. Give the goalie time to prepare for the next shooter.

European Hockey Academy © IEMS

B201 VARIATION

The basic formation is the same as in **B200**, with the players now split into two groups which leave from the other end of the line, either when the first group is finished or alternating side to side.

Teaching Points: The skaters practice cutting in and shooting from both sides and the goaltenders can work on playing angles properly. Follow the shot for a rebound and give the goalie time to prepare for the next shot.

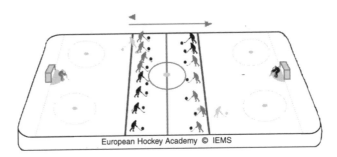

European Hockey Academy © IEMS

B202 VARIATION

The players line up in the basic **B2** formation, facing the red line with pucks. The lines should be in the neutral zone, about one stride over the blue line. One player at a time skates through the opposite line and takes a slapshot on goal, then he turns away from the goal so that he won't be hit by the next shooter. Have enough pucks so that each player can take at least two shots. Repeat until all the pucks have been shot.

Teaching Points: Practice fast starts with the puck, and shoot from between the blue line and the top of the circles. Goalkeepers must come far enough out to cut down the angles and avoid rebounds, by either deflecting the shot to the corner, smothering the rebound and shooting the puck into a safe area or catching the shot. Give and go passes to the opposite line can be added.

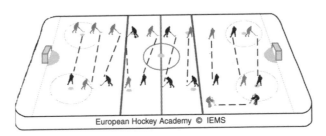

European Hockey Academy © IEMS

B3 BASIC FORMATION

The players line up, facing each other, parallel to the boards. This formation allows them to learn passing, stickhandling and puck protection skills (**B300** Variation).

Teaching Points: Begin with players close together as this is easier and allows for more passes. Gradually increase the distance between players, and have them listen to the noise made by their passing and receiving. Loud noises mean that they are slapping their passes or not absorbing the puck by giving with it when receiving a pass. When they can pass standing still they are ready to move toward each other, move forward, backward or pivot while passing or receiving.

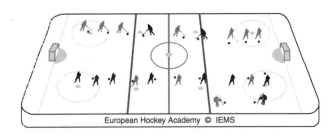

B 300 BASIC VARIATION

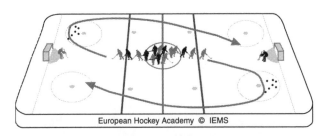

B4 BASIC FORMATION

The formation is the same as **CI** and **EI** but the purpose of the **B** exercises is to develop individual and partner skills. The players stand in a straight row in the middle of the rink with half of the players facing each goal. This formation allows for one-on-one exercises that use the full length of the ice and at the same time reduces the space in the middle. Many game-like exercises can be created that teach the player to read the game and use his skills at the proper time and place on the rink.

Teaching Points: Depending on the type of exercise, players should wait until the goalie is ready for another shot before leaving.

In search of the best hockey for young people.

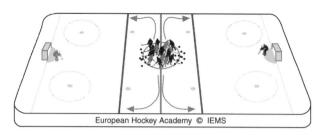

European Hockey Academy © IEMS

B5 BASIC FORMATION

The players stand in the middle face-off circle with half of the players facing each goal. One half executes the drills in one direction and the other half in the other direction. Some examples of activities are; skating toward the boards, forward or backward, or accelerating while receiving a pass at full speed.

Other tasks such as tight turns and cutting in can be added. Pucks can be placed at various spots to create more complex tasks. Shoot-ins and cycling can also be done from this formation.

Teaching Points: Practice the various individual skills as well as partner skills from this formation. This is a half-ice formation and can be used at one end while at the opposite end another type of drill may be going on.

European Hockey Academy © IEMS

B500 VARIATION

Players practice at different locations throughout the rink, either alone or in pairs.

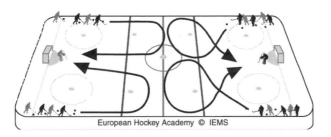

European Hockey Academy © IEMS

B6 BASIC FORMATION

This is another half-ice formation that can have many variations. The players are grouped in the corners of the rink and shoot on the goal – at either the far end or at the same end as they are standing. This formation can be used for warm-up routines before the game, and is very useful for individual as well as partner and team exercises.

Teaching Points: The shorter the skating distance, the more repetitions possible. This may be a concern for the less skilled and younger players. Depending on the task, the players come to the same row or switch sides.

European Hockey Academy © IEMS

B600 VARIATION

In this formation, individual skills are practiced using four groups standing along the boards, either at the blue line or in the neutral zone.

Teaching Points: In situations using one or two players, the skaters from two lines can leave at the same time. When three or more players are involved it works best if skaters from only one line leave at the same time.

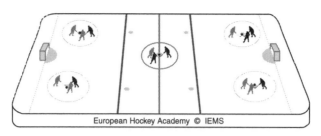

European Hockey Academy © IEMS

B7 FACEOFF PRACTICE

Practice taking faceoffs at the dots on the various zones of the ice. One player drops the puck while two players practice faceoff techniques.

Teaching Points: The player should watch the puck in the referee's hand. Another habit to develop is to check that all players are in position and ready before putting the stick down for a faceoff.

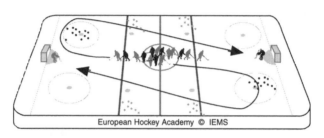

European Hockey Academy © IEMS

C1 BASIC FORMATION

C coded exercises take the individual skills learned in the **A** exercises, and the partner skills learned in **B** exercises, and put them into more game-like situations. In **C** exercises the main purpose is to score while on offense and to prevent a goal, and regain possession of the puck while defending. In **C1** the players are lined up in a row in the neutral zone with each half facing the goal on their half of the ice. This is the same basic formation as in **B4** and **E1**. The players leave the line, skating toward their own net, and turn the other way at the faceoff circle, or else shoot on the net and then get another puck. Each line turns toward the other side of the rink. Different game-like tasks are done while skating toward the opposite net.

Teaching Points: This formation can be used for **A** and **B** drills and can then progress into more complex **C** exercises.

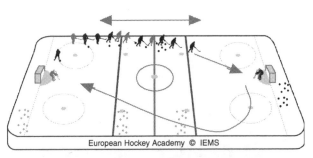

European Hockey Academy © IEMS

C2 BASIC FORMATION

In this formation all of the players line up on one side of the rink, against the boards. This formation is good when large groups leave at the same time. If only one or two players leave at a time, the lineup is too long, unless it is used for timing or speed purposes. Usually **C2** exercises start with a shot on goal, followed by picking up a new puck and playing a game-like situation, such as a breakout or a two-on-two, or three-on-one etc.

Teaching Points: This formation gives maximum space for the drills. Adjust where you want the players to stand. If the exercise requires space in the neutral zone, then have them line up inside the blue line. If the area inside the blue line is needed, then line up in the neutral zone. As a coach you have to decide what is important to make your **C** drills as game like as possible. Almost all of the essential skills of hockey can be practiced from the **C2** formation. Practicing the challenges of game-like situations, like breakouts and timing, are important in developing the players' ability to use their skills at the right place and time during a game.

European Hockey Academy © IEMS

C3 BASIC FORMATION

The players are in two groups, against the boards on opposite sides of the ice. The players can start out in many ways, such as making an offensive play and taking a shot at one end, and then picking up a new puck and making a play at the other end. They can also practice team play activities, such as the break-out or other situations such as a five-on-zero followed by a three-on-two or, four-on-one, the other way. All the drill situations can be practiced from this formation, with the advantage that the players must make game-like read and react decisions in all three zones.

Teaching Points: The coach can have the players practice a particular individual or team skill at any area on the ice. The coach can concentrate on one skill while his assistants are at another area focusing on another aspect of the drill. Move the lineup along the boards. When the neutral zone is important, keep the players inside the blue line and close to the boards. Move them closer to the red line if the deep zone play is the focus.

DI BASIC FORMATION

D coded exercises are the most important part of the teaching system, because they involve the game itself. The other exercises all lead up to the **D** exercises as building blocks for learning how to play in game-like situations.

Teaching Points: DI uses the whole ice with two nets. The traditional and natural way of learning by "scrimmages" is used, but rule variations enable the coach to use the ice more effectively.

D2 BASIC FORMATION

Games are played cross-ice with nets, pylons, lines on boards, etc. as the goals. Special rules allow the players to practice individual- or team-play skills in this smaller area. In this formation many game understanding, reading and reacting skills will naturally be developed. This formation encourages creativity and split vision in more realistic situations.

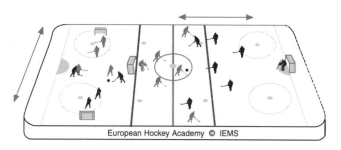

European Hockey Academy © IEMS

D3 BASIC FORMATION

In the **D3** formation, the ice surface is used by combining **D1** in two zones and **D2** in one zone. This formation is very useful if the skill levels or size of the players varies. More advanced players can use **D1**, while the others play in **D2** formation. This formation is very helpful when one end is needed to practice skills which don't have much movement. Games can go on in two zones; techniques can be taught in the other zone.

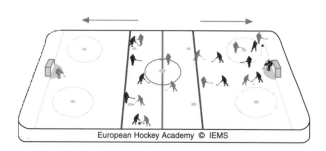

European Hockey Academy © IEMS

D4 FORMATION

In the **D4** formation the players either use one-third or one-half of the rink. In order to go onto offense, the defense must carry the puck over the blue line and then turn back into the zone. If half of the rink is available, the defense must carry the puck as far as the red line before turning back. All players must be onside in these games. This rule promotes skating and much more realistic playing situations.

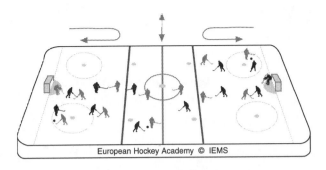

European Hockey Academy © IEMS

D400 VARIATION

A game at each end, with one goal, and a cross-ice game in the middle.

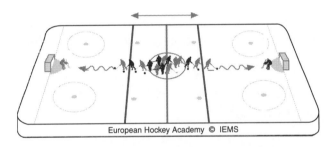

European Hockey Academy © IEMS

E1 BASIC FORMATION

These exercises are meant to give the team a good way to finish the practice. The formation is the same as **B4** and **C1**.

Teaching Points: Team contests, like a shootout, where players take penalty shots are fun for the shooters and the goalies. Prizes for the winners or push ups, etc., for the losers add intensity and enjoyment to this cool-down exercise. For variation, sometimes have the winners do pushups.

QUALITY ICE-HOCKEY TRAINING

The quality of ice-hockey training can be measured by how much the players improve. To achieve this improvement, the coach must set realistic goals and plan practices that have high activity.

When on the ice, it is also important to do, **the right things, the right way, in the right place.**

Be it right or wrong, players get good at what they practice, so it is very important to work on good techniques. For example, if players don't focus on hitting the net during scoring practice, they are only getting good at missing the net.

It is important to work on the essentials of the game, such as facing the puck, changing speed, good individual techniques, keeping the defensive side, etc.

In the final analysis, the effectiveness of a practice is demonstrated in how well the player and the team play. If the individuals and the team play better, the team also wins more games.

Teaching Modules As A Tool For The Coach

The teaching modules have been designed to help the players and the coach learn hockey in a natural way. The individual and team skills have been put into practice modules that follow a logical progression. The modules will help the players master the skills as well as teach the coach how to run a quality practice. For example, after completing the skating exercises, the players will have mastered the proper skating posture and be able to move on ice in all directions. The coach will have mastered how to organize the players on the ice and will be confident in his ability to run a quality ice-hockey practice.

HOW TO TEACH THE SYSTEM

1 How old are the players?

Children and adults learn and behave differently during practice. Older players are able to listen to instructions, while a good demonstration is the best teacher for children. The rule to follow is, **the younger the player, the less verbal the instruction.**

2 How many players are there?

It is possible to run a successful skating practice for 120 players at the same time. When there are large groups of players on the ice at once, the tasks must be simple and few. Some methods for handling many players are dividing the rink into working areas, working in groups, or having stations and rotate. There is a lot of room on the ice if the coach is flexible.

3 What is the skill level?

When planning a practice, the coach must use exercises that suit the skill level of the players. **Too simple bores and too difficult frustrates,** is a principle to follow. Designing practices that challenge and improve, as well as stimulate players to focus on the exercises, is a very important coaching skill.

4 What time is the practice?

Late in the evening or after a weekend tournament the players are tired and have difficulty learning new things. When the players are tired it is better to do simple exercises. Play a lot of games and stress activity and enjoyment. On a cold outdoor rink, organize a game where everyone plays and, if the ice is too snowy, use balls instead of pucks.

5 How many pucks?

For the teaching system to work with maximum activity, there should be at least one puck for each player. When shooting drills are done, two pucks per player keeps the drills going.

6 How many coaches?

The formations run themselves, when simple guidelines are given by the coach. Coaches can be located in different areas of the ice where teaching can be done.

7 How many goalies?

Most drills are designed with at least two goalies in mind. However, many times there may be one or even no goalie. The goalies are active in the system and are a part of most exercises. When goalies are missing, the nets may be turned around to face the end or, even better, by lying them face down and only allowing a goal if the shot hits the top netting, if there is any metal hit the goal doesn't count. Small nets and pylons can also be used. In the warm-up, the goalies can do the same skating exercises as the other players at the beginning, followed by special goalie skating routines in the crease area.

8 How much practice time is there?

The length of **A-B-C-D-E** sessions depend on the ice time available. Players should stretch before going on the ice and the coach should do most of his talking in the dressing room. The ice is for moving and practicing hockey, not for activities that can be done other places. If there isn't much ice time it is better to do fewer activities and leave time for the **D** games, instead of rushing through and trying to do too much.

9 How much ice is available?

Sometimes the coach has only part of the rink to use. Most of the exercises can also be executed cross-ice. By having extra goals or boards to split the rink, it is possible for more players to practice or for two teams to have an extra practice.

10 Discipline!

Last but not least **discipline**. When the coach signals or whistles, the players must come to him right away. Younger players should listen by going down on one knee, so fooling around and distractions can be kept to a minimum. By trying to foresee problems before they occur, the coach can avoid spending valuable ice time dealing with poor behavior.

QUESTIONS THE COACH MUST ASK HIM/HERSELF

When teaching a player or a team, the coach must constantly keep these questions in mind.

1. **What am I going to do?**

2. **Why am I doing it?**

3. **When should I do it?**

4. **Where is the best place to do it?**

5. **How will I do it?**

Learning to be a coach is similar to learning to be a player. Just as a player needs about 10,000 repetitions to learn a slapshot, the coach must realize that it takes time to learn to run good practices.

The repetitions of the basic formations and exercises in the **A-B-C-D-E** system offer many variations that teach the player how to play and the coach how to coach.

The **A-B-C-D-E** system is organized in seven levels of progression. In the beginning, the coach should stick to the system and add some of his or her own variations later.

There is a systematic, logical progression of the individual and team skills from level 0 (non-skaters) up to level 6.

Individual skills have been put into modules on coaching cards, which are coded with a letter for the formation and a number for the exercise. When one level is finished, there are skill tests that must be done before moving to the next level.

THE SEVEN QUALITY ICE-PRACTICE LEVELS

This material has been coded into levels from zero to six. These levels follow a progression from the simple to the more complex. The levels are designed to help the coach choose the activities that are appropriate for the age and skill level of his players.

Level 0

This includes **A1** modules one to six for skating instruction, where beginners learn to move on the ice by doing balance and lead-up skating exercises.

D games and contests are also used here to increase the enjoyment and create situations where the newly learned skills are practiced.

Level 1

Skating school includes games and contests. The idea of this level is for the players to be able to move in all directions with and without the puck.

The first offensive role, being able to carry the puck with your head up, is emphasized. There is no need to teach passing, receiving and shooting at this level of player development. It is better to learn to skate and carry the puck and then play games. Falling and getting up, while playing, is a good exercise too. During the modified games, young players experience the need to learn more advanced skills. This makes them more receptive later, when these skills are introduced. Any skill taught that doesn't relate to personal experience and fulfill individual needs will have no meaning for the players.

Level 2

The first and second playing roles are emphasized and the third and fourth playing roles are introduced. Level two includes: stick/puckhandling, shooting, passing, one-on-one school, and games and contests. This level teaches the players the necessary concepts for stickhandling and goalie techniques, and the concepts of the offensive and defensive one-on-one. At level two some fundamental team play concepts are introduced, such as recognizing whether you are the first, second, third, fourth or fifth player closest to the puck, or to your net, and making the decision whether you are playing forward or defense. Many modified games, with passing rules, are used to make the players conscious of where they are on the ice and who is with them. Two-on-two situations are used extensively, with all of the playing roles.

Level 3

The first and second playing roles are worked on at a more advanced level. Level three includes: intermediate passing, receiving, skating, shooting, angling, and defensive-side school as well as games and contests that practice these skills. Puckhandling with the head up, seeing the puck at all times, always playing the man while in one-on-one defensive situations, are the basic individual skills needed before team-play skills can be developed. The four playing roles up to the three-on-three situation are the focus of the team play teaching.

Level 4

The individual skills of the first and second playing roles are practiced at an advanced level, with body-checking skills being emphasized The third playing role of offensive support is emphasized in team play practice. The players are now skilled enough to work on more advanced team play. Power-play systems can be introduced and players become more specialized in their positions. Game situations have more transitional play, where the players must read and react to the situation.

Level 5

This is an advanced level, where the individual skills of playing roles one and two are practiced for warm-up and review. Role four, with defensive team play, is the emphasis in Level five. Penalty killing systems can become more elaborate. Concentrate also on power plays and offensive and defensive team play.

Level 6

In level six, all of the individual skills in roles one and two, and team play skills of roles three and four are practiced. Transition is emphasized with the rule: **You must attack so that you can defend and defend so that you can attack.** Everything must be done very quickly. The skills must be practiced at as close to game speed as possible. Games are used that emphasize transition and "read and react" skills, so that the players recognize immediately what playing role they are in and know what to do.

SAMPLES OF TEACHING MODULES
Cards

Hockey Coaching:
The ABCs of International Hockey
Juhani Wahlsten – Tom Molloy

1 | Level 0 | SKATING

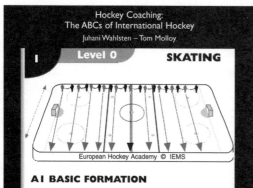

European Hockey Academy © IEMS

A1 BASIC FORMATION

Description:
The players are lined up along the side boards. The exercises are done with either 1 or 2 groups.
A1-0000

Teaching points:
A1 is the most basic of all the formations, and is used first in the teaching system, because the skating distance is short.

Divide the players into small groups according to the colors of their jersey or simply number the players so that they have room to maneuver without colliding with another player. When the first group has reached the opposite boards, then the next group leaves. Repeat the same methods when going the other way.

Hockey Coaching:
The ABCs of International Hockey
Juhani Wahlsten – Tom Molloy

2 | Level 0 | SKATING

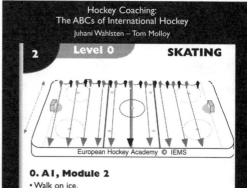

European Hockey Academy © IEMS

0. A1, Module 2

- Walk on ice.
- Walk and glide on 2 skates.
- Walk and glide on 2 skates with knees bent over toes.
- Stationary jumps on 2 skates.
- Snowplough skate by toeing out and then toeing in with both skates at once.
- Snowplough stop by sitting low and pushing the inner skate edges into the ice.
- Run on ice and snowplough stop.
- Toe-in toe-out skate, using the right skate to cut a "C" into the ice and the left leg to steer.
- Toe-in toe-out skate, using the left skate to cut a "C" into the ice and the right leg to steer – toe-in toe-out skate, alternating feet, the sequence is stroke-glide, stroke with other skate-glide.
- Flat-footed toe-in toe-out skate and then glide on 1 foot.
- T-push followed by glide.   A1-0003

Hockey Coaching:
The ABCs of International Hockey
Juhani Wahlsten – Tom Molloy

3 | Level 0 | SKATING

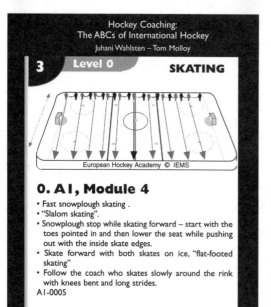

European Hockey Academy © IEMS

0. A1, Module 4

- Fast snowplough skating.
- "Slalom skating".
- Snowplough stop while skating forward – start with the toes pointed in and then lower the seat while pushing out with the inside skate edges.
- Skate forward with both skates on ice, "flat-footed skating"
- Follow the coach who skates slowly around the rink with knees bent and long strides.
A1-0005

Hockey Coaching:
The ABCs of International Hockey
Juhani Wahlsten – Tom Molloy

4 | Level 0 | SKATING

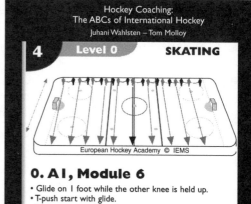

European Hockey Academy © IEMS

0. A1, Module 6

- Glide on 1 foot while the other knee is held up.
- T-push start with glide.
- Push a partner down the ice.
- "Flat footed skating", skate forward with both skates on ice.
- Glide on 1 skate.
- Glide on 1 skate with the other knee raised.
- Thrust and push with 1 skate while gliding on the other.
- Skate forward and do a 1-foot gliding stop by extending 1 skate in front and sitting low with knees bent and scraping the ice in front by turning the blade toward the middle so the inside edge is pushing against the ice.
- Skate backward and do a 1-foot stop by extending 1 skate behind and sitting low with knees bent and scrape the ice behind by turning the blade toward the outside so the inside edge is pushing against the ice.
A1-0007

MODULES,

·

CARDS, LEVELS

The following modules represent the typical exercises used at these specific levels.

LEVELS 0 to 1

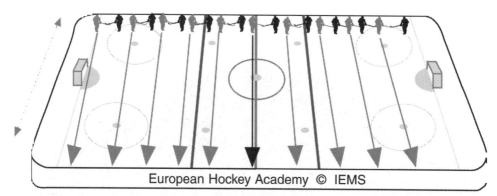

European Hockey Academy © IEMS

0.A1, MODULE 1

- skating posture in forward skating
- standing on the inside edge of the skates
- standing on the outside edge of the skates
- standing on one skate

- standing on one skate and kicking back and forth
- standing on one skate and kicking side to side across the body
- pushing a chair or large pylon
- walking on skates

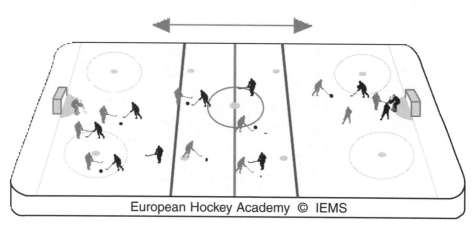

European Hockey Academy © IEMS

PLAYING WITH 7 PUCKS

Two teams gather at center ice and the coach drops seven pucks. The first team to score four goals wins, and another game begins. Make sure that there are only seven pucks and the pucks are left in the net after a goal.

LEVELS 1 to 2

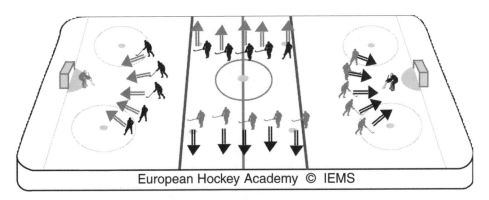

European Hockey Academy © IEMS

B1 MODULE 1

- stationary shooting at the boards or net using the sweepshot

- stationary shooting at a target on the boards using a backhand

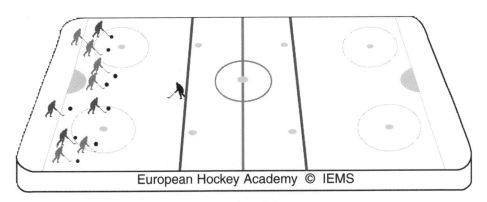

European Hockey Academy © IEMS

BRITISH PUCK DOG

The players line up behind the goal line, each player has a puck; when the player in the middle yells British Puck Dog all the players carry their pucks, trying to get to the end without being checked. If a player loses his puck he remains in the middle to check. The last player with a puck wins.

LEVELS 2

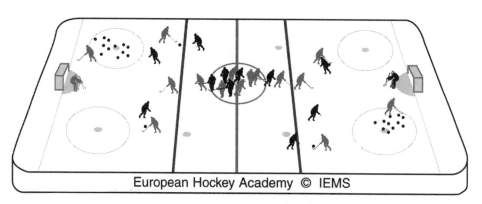

European Hockey Academy © IEMS

C1, MODULE 1
1 ON 1, DEFENSEMAN WITHOUT STICK

The players are lined up in the basic **C1** formation. Pucks are placed behind the face-off dots at each end. One-on-one, the defenseman without his stick or with his stick held upside down.

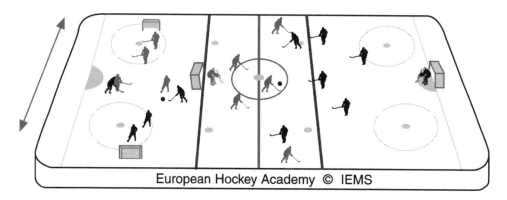

European Hockey Academy © IEMS

D3
GAME WITH THE PUCKCARRIER TAKING AT LEAST THREE QUICK STRIDES BEFORE PASSING

This is a game requiring at least one pass. The puckcarrier, however, must take three quick strides before passing or shooting.

LEVELS 2 to 3

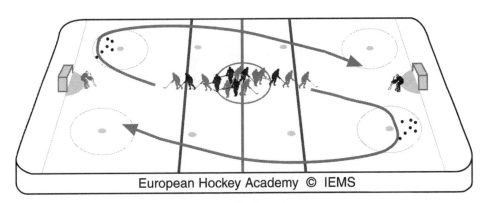

European Hockey Academy © IEMS

B4 MODULE 2

B4, 02
- skating while always seeing the puck that is placed on the center faceoff dot, "skating/movement routines".
- forward
- backward
- crossover forward
- crossover backward
- pivots on the circles and lines

- tight turns on the lines and "the walls"

B4, 03
- mirror your partner's forward skating while skating backwards

B4, 04
- follow the leader while skating forward

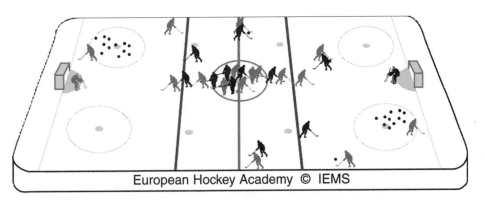

European Hockey Academy © IEMS

C1, 03 1 ON 1, FORECHECKING

The players are lined up in the basic **C1** formation. Pucks are placed behind the face-off dots at each end. The first skater picks up the puck and turns towards the strong side (the side where the puck is) boards, the second skater delays, then forechecks.

LEVELS 3 to 4

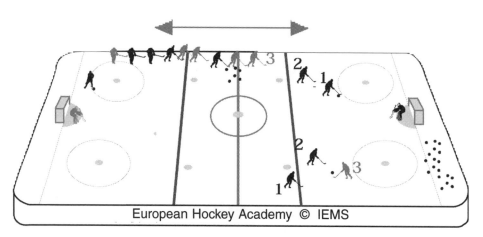

European Hockey Academy © IEMS

C2, MODULE 5, 1 ON 2

Three players leave from the **C2** formation. Number one shoots and rebounds. The player picks up a new puck and carries it down against numbers two and three, who are playing as defense and want to stop number one before their blue line. The defender on the puck side should close the gap and make contact, while the other defender swings behind and picks up a loose puck, or plays one-on-one if the first defender is beaten. This technique eliminates the risk of two defenders playing one attacker, while a late offensive player joins the play and has a breakaway.

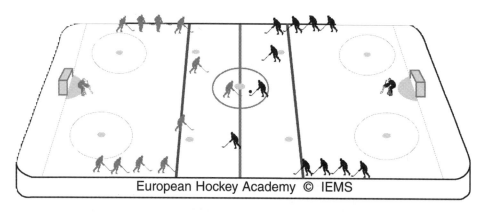

European Hockey Academy © IEMS

2 ON 2, 3 ON 3, FULL ICE GAMES

Playing in small groups for 30 second shifts is a good way to practice support on offense and defense.

LEVELS 4 to 5

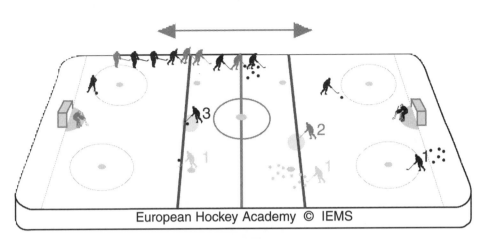

European Hockey Academy © IEMS

C2, MODULE 3,
3 ON 0, FLYING ATTACKS

This exercise combines the timing practiced in the other **C2** drills. Three players leave; number one shoots, looks for a rebound, then picks up a new puck in the corner. Number two saves ice (slows down) and asks for a pass in the high slot area. Number two now carries the puck over the blue line, while number three has timed his\skating from the wide wing and asks for a pass at the offensive blue line. Number one and two both pick up new pucks and shoot on goal.

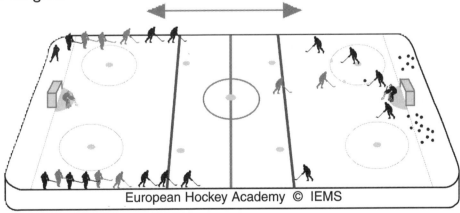

European Hockey Academy © IEMS

C3, MODULE 6
BREAKOUT 5 ON 2

The players are lined up in **C3** formation, but now two forecheckers defend against the breakout situation. The pucks are shot or picked up from behind the net or from the corners.

LEVELS 5 to 6

AN EXAMPLE OF A GAME METHOD

Here is an example of the games method of teaching, using two teams of ten players each. The number of players on the ice at one time may vary.

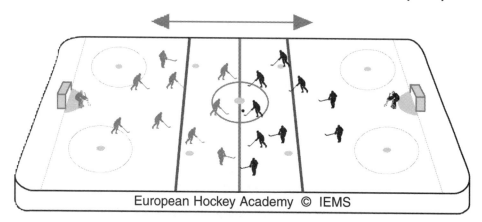

European Hockey Academy © IEMS

- **Play a regulation game of 10 versus 10.**
- **Split the teams into two lines of 5 versus 5.**
- **Split the teams into three lines of 3+3+4 versus 3+3+4.**
- **Split the teams into four lines of 2+3+2+3 versus 2+3+2+3.**
- **Split the teams into five lines of 2+2+2+2+2 versus 2+2+2+2+2.**
- **Split the teams into ten lines of 1+1+1+1+1+1+1+1+1+1 versus 1+1+1+1+1+1+1+1+1+1.**

EPILOGUE

The principles in playing a net or goal-oriented team game like ice hockey don´t change. The more we have studied the game the more we are convinced that the following principles are fundamental to successful coaching:

- **Keep things simple,**
- **Stick with the system and the process of the system will take care of teaching the game.**

The basic ice patterns we have outlined are like the basic chords in music. Once learned it is easy to compose your own practices. Good luck!

After learning this basic system the coach has the necessary understanding to enable him to run a good practice. He can take the principles of the teaching system and expand them with his own ideas to meet the needs of this team.

PART II

•

UNDERSTANDING AND LEARNING THE GAME

UNDERSTANDING AND LEARNING THE GAME

*"Without an understanding of
the game there are no
right decisions made."*

A player can develop individual skills by playing "shinny" with his friends. When the same player joins a competitive team the player must learn how to cooperate with his team mates in offensive and defensive situations. It is the coaches' role to organize the practice that develops both skills and team play

To be able to do, this a coach has to have a picture of how he wants the team to play the game. He must have a clear understanding of the basic principles of hockey and the coaching techniques needed to teach them to his players.

CONCEPTS AND TERMS

The Game

The game is the coordinated movement of the puck and players, with the simple goals of scoring and preventing the other team from scoring.

Game - the way it works

The opening faceoff is the first loose puck situation. Winning loose pucks means that the team can score and that the opposition can't.

Movement

The players on the ice are either creating or restricting movement by continuous moves and counter moves during the game. Other factors may include rules and the time left in the game. As Anatoli Tarasov said "the puck has no lungs, it does not get tired", in other words, **the players who understand the game can eliminate unnecessary work by supporting each other, by taking care of their own playing role, and letting the puck do much of the work.**

Everything that happens on the ice occurs in one of these three situations:

0 The puck is loose and neither team has it.

1 Your team has the puck on offense.

2 The other team has the puck, putting your team on defense.

Game Philosophy

Game philosophy is simply a combination of all the other points. It is the way the coach and the players view the game. Each coach and player has a philosophy of how the game should be played in order to get the best results. It is a personal "truth of the game."

Coaching Philosophy

Coaching philosophy is the coach and her coaching staff's understanding of the game and the best way to develop the players.

Player Roles

The hockey player must read the play with her player role in mind. The player must be ready to play with the puck or without it, to play offense or to play defense.

The four player roles are:

On Offense:
- The player has the puck.
- The player supports the puckcarrier.

On Defense:
- One player checks the puckcarrier.
- The other players support by covering other offensive players.

Understanding the Game – "HOCKEY SENSE"

Understanding the game is the player's ability to comprehend how the game works – the principles of the game and the movement. The player must learn to make decisions in the game which are favorable for the team in all the various offensive, defensive and transitional moments of the game. Both the coach and the players must understand the goals of the game and the tools needed to achieve these goals. They should understand positional play and how to play with and without the puck, as well as how the offensive and defensive game are tied to each other. When this understanding is achieved, the players can change roles to deal with the various play situations by changing tactics during the game.

Reading the Game

The ability to read the game becomes important when, instead of just one player, the entire unit attacks and defends together. Reading the game is the ability to understand and observe the location of teammates and the opponents, as well as the puck and the speed and direction of the play. It is the anticipation of the next play. In short, it is **to be at the right place at the right time in offensive, defensive and loose puck situations.**

THE PLAYER´S ROLES

Playing with or without the puck

In a good team everyone plays both offense and defense, with or without the puck. In offense the players create space for the puck carrier by screening, picking, and breaking to openings for the pass. A good offense always gives the puck carrier two safe, low-risk passes; the last player is never left with the puck. All three lanes, and low, medium and high depths are used on the attack.

Most of the game is played without the puck. Solid individual offensive and defensive skills give the player more "tools"to be successful during the game. These individual tools include: puck-handling, passing, shooting on offense, as well as defensive skills to check with and without the puck.

The defensive skills are critical to gain possession of the puck, but the keys to a productive game, where the puck can be used to advantage, are the puck control skills of stick– and puck-handling, passing, and receiving.

The most important player on defense is the player who checks the puck carrier. His movement is the key to how his teammates defend the play. If he is aggressive, his teammates defend by close man-to-man coverage; if the first checker is passive, his teammates cover lanes and areas of the ice.

The actions of the puck carrier on offense are the key to how his offensive teammates must react in their supporting roles.

Once more, if the offensive players, without the puck, do not create openings, then the puck carrier can only protect the puck or look for open space. On defense, any hesitation of the closest checker or neglect of defensive responsibilities makes regaining the puck more difficult.

PLAYER'S CO-OPERATION

Prerequisites

The precondition for a workable game plan is a disciplined approach to positional play, an understanding of the playing roles and teamwork.

Each player on the team must be committed to perform the commonly agreed upon tasks to the best of his ability. Team performance improves only when this simple concept is followed.

When the team has good puck-control skills and good organization on the ice, it saves a lot of energy on defense, in trying to regain the puck, and creates many opportunities to score.

On offense, the main idea is to get on the offensive side of the defender in the slot area in front of the net. On defense, the main idea is to steer the player to the outside lanes, while staying on the "defensive side" between the puck and the net. Good defensive players are patient in letting the opponent make the first move, then steering the play wide away from their net. Good puck control itself is part of good defense because the opponent cannot score if he doesn't have the puck. A good hockey player masters both the offensive and defensive plays.

Learning to Read and React

In modern hockey the concept of "reading the game" is basic. When a coach understands the concept and has transmitted it to his players, there is a basis for interpreting changing game situations and reacting productively; thus play improves.

The coach must not only work on the individual and team skills, but also on thinking skills. **Without an understanding of the game there are no right decisions made, and without physical skills the decisions cannot be carried out.** The most natural way to develop "read and react skills" is simply to play many kinds of net-centered games. Mini games with modified rules are a good way to teach the players to be in the right place at the right time.

When the coach understands the principles of the "ideal game", he has the precondition to teach his players the ideal way to play. To do this they must have common terms for all aspects of the game.

NUMBERING AS A COMMUNICATION TOOL

To avoid misunderstanding, numbering the players according to the situation is a great tool to teach read and react skills. Number the three phases of the game, and their description, with numbers 0-1-2. Numbering the different phases of the game makes the communication easier and prevents confusion at the verbal level.

THE ABC OF READING THE GAME – 0-1-2

The three phases of the game can be described by the numbers as follows:

0 **Zero Game**

Neither team has the puck and it is loose. The decisions players make in these situations create or deny successful transition from offense to defense or from defense to offense. We will be referring to this situation as "Number 0" or "0 Game".

1. **Number One Game**

"Your team has the puck." Your players are attacking and they can score. This phase of the game is described with number "1". We will be referring to this situation as "Number 1" or "Number 1 Game."

2. **Number Two Game**

"The opponent has the puck." The team is playing defense, preventing the opponent from scoring. This situation is described as "Number 2" or "number 2 game."

During these three frequently changing phases the players must read and react. The way to react depends on the players' positions in relation to the puck and closeness to their own net. The golden rule of interpreting any game situation is that the player has to face the play in order to see the situation, then she can react. Turning her back to the play is a cardinal mistake.

The closest player's reaction to a loose puck (0) determines what is the next play to be made (1-2). Does the team have a chance to score or not. The statistics have shown that the team that wins the most "zero games" usually wins the game. Teams should concentrate on winning these loose pucks to improve their won-lost record. Although this all appears simple on paper, to teach effective transition thinking, and make it a team habit, takes a lot of effort and practice.

Numbering as a Communicating Tool Between the Players

Both in offense and defensive games, the moves of the players are determined by what roles they are playing, and the roles are determined by their closeness to the puck and whether they are in a 0-1-2 playing situation.

Numbering is a great aid to teach the players read and react skills, so that they know their playing roles:

Role One – The first attacker, the puck carrier" – number one (1).

Role Two – The other offensive players support the puck carrier by getting open for a pass, screening or giving width and depth to the attack – number two (2).

Role Three – The closest checker to the opponent – number three (3).

Role Four – The other defensive players cover man-to-man or an area of the ice. All maintain the defensive side and steer the attack to the outside – number four (4). Depending on the distance from the puck, and whether he is the third, fourth, or fifth player closest to the puck, the player in the fourth playing role must support by covering an opponent, switching, or double-teaming.

Discipline – The Key for Read and React

The space on the ice will be utilized best in the game when each of the players does his own job. Then the game does not proceed by accident, but instead on an understanding of the game. This understanding makes reading, reacting and playing the four roles easier, (reading the phases 0-1-2 or the roles 1-2-3-4). A disciplined system starts with a solid defensive game as the basis on which to create transition into a good offensive game.

Numbering according the Players' Closeness to the Play

The movement of the player in the course of the game, as well the communication between the coach and the player, gets easier using the numbers. The position and the role can be defined, e.g., by the proximity to the play and the position on the ice, using the lines, dots, goals, etc. of the rink.

Numbering players will help, for example, when playing a triangle in the offensive zone. The players are numbered according to the order in which they pass the offensive blue line.

1. Number one (1)

The first player to skate over the blue line.

2. Number two (2)

The second player to skate over the blue line, and drives to the net.

3. Number three (3)

The third player who skates over the blue line, and trails and completes the triangle, (1-2-3 principle)

When learning the system of play, the players are numbered. For example, in the breakout, the first player to initiate the breakout (in most cases a defenseman) is number one (1), the second player supports from the front of the net (2), the third player back goes to the strong side boards (3), the fourth player protects the middle lane and mirrors the puck (4), the fifth player goes to the weak side boards (5).

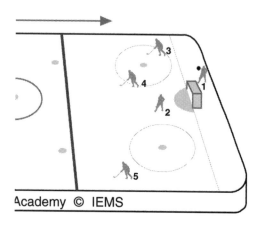

Academy © IEMS

To read the game, in the defensive zone, again use the 1-2-3 principle which is determined by the players' closeness to the puck and to the net.

1. Number one (1)

The player who plays the puck carrier.

2. Number two (2)

The player who checks the opponents driving the net, number 2, the number two defensive player protects the front of the net.

3. Number three (3)

The third player who comes into the defensive zone and plays the opponents' number 3.

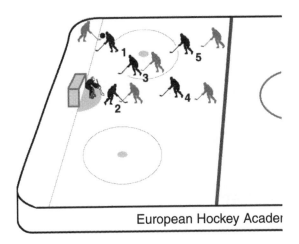

European Hockey Academ

HOW TO SEE THE GAME AS A COACH

The more the coach understands the game, the more he sees.

The more the coach understands the game, the more he sees what is really happening on the ice. He is able to tell the difference between the essential and the trivial. The coach has to know the basic principles of the game and how the players must cooperate in order to play in a positive manner. To read the game as a coach there is a basic check list that he must go through when analyzing his team's play. To start with, the coach should watch how the players perform in the four player roles:

1 **Player with the puck**

2 **Player supporting the puckcarrier**

3 **Player checking the puckcarrier**

4 **Player covering the players or an area away from the puck**

All of these roles must be carried out in the three phases of the game:

"0" **Loose puck situation**

"1" **We have the puck - offense**

"2" **The opponent has the puck – defense**

0 **"Zero Game" - Loose Puck Situation:**

Does the player recognize that he will be on offense or defense and, when the situation is not clear, does he recognize whether his role and distance from his net allow him to make an offensive or a defensive decision?

1 **"One Game"**

The player is on offense with his team in possession of the puck.

2 **"Two Game"**

The player is on defense and the other team has the puck.

The player has to see the puck in order to react to the play situation. On defense the player must constantly look at the puck, and see the player he is covering. A common term is to "keep his head on a swivel", looking back and forth. A good technique is to point one shoulder at the puck and one at the offensive player you are covering, constantly keeping eye contact with the puck and the offensive player.

LOOSE PUCK GAME

The reaction of the closest player dictates whether the team will be on offense or on defense.

Face-offs: The first thought of all players should be defensive, until they can read the situation better. The player who takes the face-off should set up where the other players line up.

All players must know their role in the face-off in all three possible situations:

- **Win**
- **Lose**
- **Draw**

How the Player Plays "Loose Puck Situations"
- Does the closest player beat the opponent to the puck and protect it with his body?
- Does the player control the opponent's stick so he can't make a play?
- Do the players use good technique so they don't take unnecessary penalties?
- Do the players drive skate to free ice when they get the puck?

OFFENSIVE GAME

Points the coach should look for:

Does everybody join the offensive attack?

All players should support the puck on offense and join the attack. The more support the puckcarrier has the more options he has. The puckcarrier should always have two safe passes to make; the other two players can spread the defense and give width and depth to the attack.

- Do the players follow their pass by supporting the new puckcarrier and getting open for a return pass?

- Do the defensemen jump into the play and give more passing options for the attack and regroups?

After transition does the first puckcarrier quickly initiate a new attack?

Modern hockey is a game of transition. Most goals are scored when a new attack is started, within the first two or three seconds after a turnover. This is because it takes that long to reorganize the defense after losing the puck. A quick offense attacks an unorganized defense, while a slow developing offense attacks an organized defense.

The first player (1) either beats his checker and carries the puck up the ice, or passes the puck (1 → 2) to the closest supporting player. The first player on the puck and the supporting player are the keys to quick transition. The players without the puck must create passing options, or the puckcarrier is forced to keep moving with the puck in order to create space and time for herself.

Do the players create width and depth in the offense?

Two forwards on the boards and the fourth and fifth players follow the attack.

The width of the attack is determined by how far apart the players in the outside lanes are. The depth of the attack is the distance between the first and fifth closest player to the puck.

- Is the offensive line spread out using all three lanes in the attack?
- Is the attack staggered, and does it end up in a triangle with one and two going to the net and the third player trailing?
- Do the players switch and continuously fill the three lanes?
- Do the defensemen play staggered in offense?

Does the offensive team take the puck into the middle lane, "to the big ice"?

Short passes increase control of the game. Passing in all directions is possible from the middle lane.

Hard long passes across the ice are effective in isolating players in 1 on 1 situations, thus enabling them to penetrate the offensive zone. These long passes can be very dangerous, if intercepted by the defenders who will counter-attack and create outnumbered situations.

Long vertical passes aren't as dangerous because the puck is still in front of the players.

• Does the puckcarrier always have one or two easy outlet passes?

• Does the pass receiver have a chance to make a second play, or is there usually a turnover?

Do the first attacks end up with a shot on goal?

• Toward the goal.

• The goalie is screened.

• Underneath the knees, preferably on the stick side.

• They make lateral passes for one-time shots.

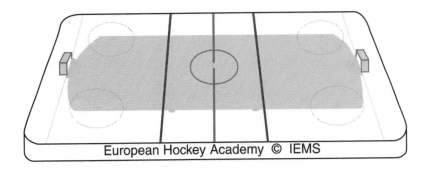

European Hockey Academy © IEMS

THE BIG ICE

In hockey 80% of the goals come after a rebound or deflection. Most goalies can make the first save if they see the shot. In other words, at least two players are needed to score. It is important to concentrate on what happens after the first shot on goal.

TRANSITION FROM OFFENSE TO DEFENSE

Does the team come back hard into its own end?

Backchecking is the key to successful hockey teams. Most goals are the result of quick transition from offense to defense. The team that backchecks can defend the line in every zone and often outnumber the attackers. Players are then close enough to receive a quick transition pass after a turnover and have enough speed to turn up ice with the puck.

On shoot-ins the forecheckers are easily screened and the puck is quickly recovered for the counterattack. The rule is that "**the puck moves faster than any player**," however the players must skate hard to backcheck; the puck can't do this work.

Do the players "defend so that they can attack, and attack so that they can defend?"

Are both defensemen (4 – 5) and one forward (3) thinking defensively even when attacking? They must all make decisions as to when to make low-risk offensive decisions.

The players should support in all three lanes and in depths of at least three waves of attackers.

DEFENSIVE GAME

The defending team has succeeded when the puck or opponent is kept out of the defensive end, or at least forced out of the scoring slot and into the corner along the boards, or the player takes a bad angle shot.

Does the whole unit defend when the opponent has the puck?

The more players play their defensive role, the harder it is for the opponent to score.

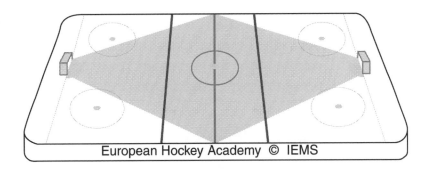

European Hockey Academy © IEMS

"DIAMOND" DEFENSIVE GAME AREA

Does the closest checking player take the space away from the opponent and does he get immediate support?

The first thing to note is how quickly the closest checking player (role 3) puts the pressure on the puck carrier and thereafter how fast he gets support from his closest teammate (role 4) and the rest of the defending players.

"The immediate pressure of the closest checker" is the key to the defensive game. His options are:
  • To gain the puck.
  • Take the man out.
  • Steer the opponent to the boards and force him to pass the puck to the desired place. Simply put; **"the goal of the defensive game is to keep the puck out of the slot area, from where goals are scored."**

THE CONCEPT OF FLOW

The "concept of flow" is common in today's offensive playing systems. This means there is a lot of cross-ice movement and switching positions in order to create scoring chances with direct and indirect attacks. The defensive players have to communicate, often switching who they cover. The key is to steer the attack wide, following the "golden rule" of defense. Stay on the defensive side between the offensive player and your own goal. In the defensive zone the game consists of stops and starts, skating straight lines and facing the puck at all times with your head on a swivel, looking alternately at the puck and at your check.

The supporting defensive player must observe the first checker. How does the the closest checking player (role 3) react? Does he create immediate pressure on the puck carrier? Does he steer the opponent towards the boards? Does he finish his check and prevent a give and go? Does he get immediate support (4), or is he out-numbered?

Does the defensive team play close to the goal and protect the middle lane?

The defending team must steer the puck out of the middle lane and, deep in the defensive zone, collapse close to the net, using the first man on the puck with a supporting box behind.

How do the defensemen play in the different zones and in their end? Do they collapse near the net or are they spread apart?

The puck carrier who is being checked by their closest defender is not the most dangerous player, the potential pass receivers are.

A good example of this is the frequent situation where the opponent's defenseman has the puck on the offensive blue line. The main job of the defenders is to clear the front of the net so the goalie can see the puck and pick up the offensive team's sticks, to prevent deflections and tip-ins.

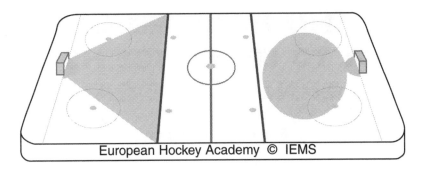

European Hockey Academy © IEMS

Using the Defensive Blue Line and the boards as an Extra Man

The offside rule, where the puck must precede the player into the zone, can be used to great advantage in the defensive game. When the puck is outside of the defensive zone, the defense is defending well. It is important to pressure the puck in order to get it outside of the blue line, and force the opposition to clear the zone to get onside.

When defending the neutral zone, force the offense to dump the puck in, or stop the attack before the blue line, then initiate a quick counter-attack.

Make sure to play the body when outnumbering the attackers at the blue line.

Try to force the play before the red line in order to cause the offense to ice the puck.

When your team clears the puck over the blue line the defensemen must hurry into the neutral zone in order to use the blue line as an extra defenseman again.

CONCLUSION

There are many "rules of thumb" for the game of ice hockey. The coach should understand the basic principles of the game in order to make her coaching ideas clearly understood. Remember – practices only have meaning if they cause the team to play better.

TRANSITIONAL THINKING:
The team should attack so they can defend and defend so they can attack

 White circles • concentrates totally on offense

 Grey circles • ready to participate either on offense or defense

 Black circles • concentrates primarily on offense

SMALL AND MODIFIED GAMES AS A TOOL TO LEARN ICE HOCKEY

"Players like to play."

The small games method signifies an alternative approach to the traditional way of running a class or practice in goal-centered games. The teaching style is a tool in learning to play. This method is based on the traditional and natural methods of pick up games and shinny. Lining up of players is avoided and the different modified games take care of teaching the rules and skills of the sport. The instructor or coach organizes the process through a progression of games. The mini-leagues and playoffs generate the situations which cause the players themselves to analyze ways to win the games. The game situations put the players into situations that they cannot handle and create a real need to know. When the players "need to know" it is time for skill drills. The techniques that are learned in the drills are now relevant to the players' needs and are in the next game progression.

The game and the roles of the players can be learned. Also, the use and the improvement of individual skills and stamina can be improved by playing small games. From a player's point of view (and this is the only view of any importance) in a normal game he always faces "small game situations". In a game he always works with one or two teammates and opponents at a time. He is always in situations of 1 on 1, 1 on 2, 2 on 1, 2 on 2, 2 on 3, 3 on 3. Players like to learn the game by playing small games. This method of practice makes sense to the players and most importantly, the team gets better. The specific goal of a hockey practice is "to learn to play better."

Small games can be played using five basic methods of using the ice. All of these methods can use two or more goals and one or more balls or pucks.

Play in one zone — play in a small area of the rink to practice movement and use of space in offense and defense. Add rules to practice individual and team thinking (playing roles) skills.

Use two or more nets, either cross or full ice — when players play on two nets they automatically learn to position themselves both in offense and defense, and react to the transition from defense to offense and vice versa.

METHODS OF USING THE RINK

Methods of using the rink in order to raise the activity ratio during the game session.

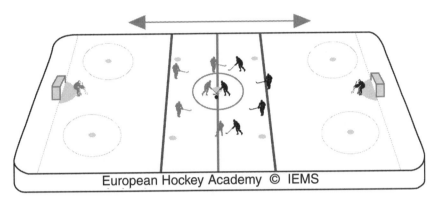

D1

Using the full playing area, one end to the other.

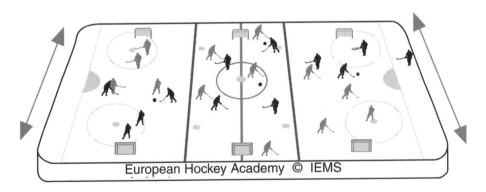

D2

Games played across the playing area with goals on the sidelines or boards.

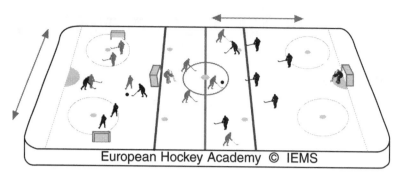

European Hockey Academy © IEMS

D3

Games going lengthwise in two zones and across inside the blue line.

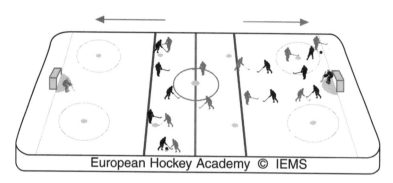

European Hockey Academy © IEMS

D4

Using half the field or rink with a goal or goals at each end, one game can be played or a game can be played on each half.

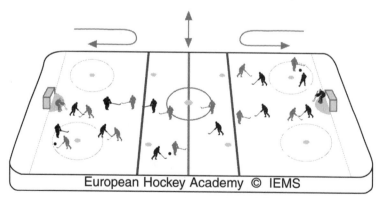

European Hockey Academy © IEMS

D400 VARIATION

A game at each end, leaving the middle area free for other activity or a cross-ice game. In this game, one or more goals are on the goal line and the rules are as in half-court basketball.

It is good to have regular methods organizing the games. Once the players get to know these game methods it will save a lot of time.

TYPES OF GAME ORGANIZATION

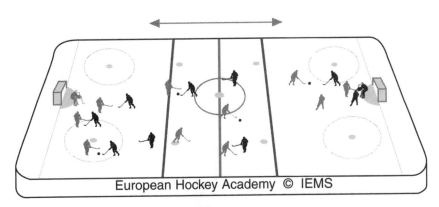

European Hockey Academy © IEMS

1

Play using more goals, nets, balls, pucks and larger teams

Using more nets, ball or pucks and larger teams allows many players, to have lots of activity and many smaller games. Rules should include no bodychecking or slapshots, and shots can only be taken when the goalie is ready. This is to prevent two shots coming at once.

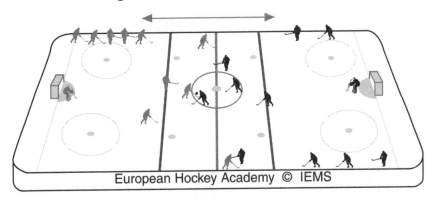

European Hockey Academy © IEMS

2

Breaking down the teams.

Two teams can be broken down into smaller units like, 1 on 1, 2 on 2, 3 on 3, 4 on 4, etc. When this is done there are two ways of creating a lot of activity.

- Time shifts and change on the whistle.
- Line up the resting players on the side; these players can give and receive passes.

A league with shorter playing time (D1, D2, D3, D4, D5)

Two teams play on a regulation field with one or more goals, but the games are shorter. Instead of playing two-20 minute periods two teams can play four-ten minute games, or eight-five minute games. This creates a league with many games, and more wins, draws and losses. It means more effort, concentration and intensity in the same amount of time.

Playoff (D1, D2, D3, D4, D5)

Two teams play a PLAYOFF FORMAT. These are similar to #2 but now you play a best two out of three, or best three out of five series, etc. The playing time can be set or else the game can end when one team scores a certain number of goals. (The first team to five goals wins). Another method is a "sudden death" game, where the game is over as soon as one team scores, or modify this and play until the other team has a two-goal lead.

GAMES METHOD ONE

Points the coach should look for:

Here is an example of the games method of teaching using two teams of 10 players each. This technique varies the number of players on at one time.

- Play a regulation game of 10 versus 10.
- Split the teams into two lines of 5 versus 5.
- Split the teams into three lines of 3+3+4 versus 3+3+4.
- Split the teams into four lines of 2+3+2+3 versus 2+3+2+3.
- Split the teams into five lines of 2+2+2+2+2 versus 2+2+2+2+2.
- Split the teams into ten lines of 1+1+1+1+1+1+1+1+1+1 versus 1+1+1+1+1+1+1+1+1+1.

GAMES METHOD TWO

Still using the example of twenty players:

Have four units of five players. Each unit is one team and the units play a round robin against the other three teams. In the first round play A versus B for one minute, while C and D rest. After one minute C plays D; A and B rest.

- Play a regulation game of 10 versus 10.

- Do this for three one minute games each. The next round will be A-D and B-C, and the third round A-C, B-D.

- The points for wins and losses are calculated. The first- and last-place teams form one team of ten players and the second and third place teams form another team of ten players.

- Now the number one game technique is used, varying the number of players are active at one time. Variations of five-on-five with active or passive spare units, such as two-on-two and three-on-three, or five, two-on-three etc.

GAMES METHOD THREE

- Use the game tables to organize leagues and tournaments.

- Form small teams and play a league with one or two pools.

- Play a two-on-two league. For example, with 20 players form five teams of two to play on one field and another group of five teams play a league on another field.

- Now the three best teams from one league play the three best from the other league in a round robin tournament (five games). The last two teams from each league play a double round robin tournament (six games each).

- When the round robin tournaments are finished, combine the winner and the last-place team into a team of four. The second and the ninth place teams join, etc. Now games can be played with five teams of four players.

Rule modifications are made depending on what the coach wants to teach. These rules force the players into the situations that build offensive and defensive team skills. These corrective games use the game itself as the teaching method.

Modified rules can also teach individual skills. For example, to teach passing, set the number of passes there must be before a goal counts. To create offensive support, restrict the number of ball//puck touches before a pass must be made. Decide that only one technique, such as the backhand, can be used. These rules make the players work on specific techniques. In passing the principle is simple. The fewer passes the more individual action. The more passes, the more team action.

By diminishing or increasing the number of passes in a game the coach teaches "read and react" as well as "space utilization" skills. Some examples of this are:

1 No passing rule – the player with the puck/ball has to beat the opponents and teammates must support by screening and breaking to openings.

2 One pass only rule – at least two players are needed. The pass receiver must try to score.

3 No give and go pass rule – this rule forces teammates to join the play and find openings. The ball/puck carrier must really look around to find the open player. In a three-on-three game, one definite player must be passed to.

4 No return pass and x number of passes combined increases the offensive support.

5 Give-and-go pass only, plus x number of passes before scoring forces players to break after passing. In more than two-on-two situations allow passing to another player after each give-and-go.

6 Only forward passing rule – teaches players to head man the ball/puck and break to openings.

7 Backward passing only – teaches trailer and drop passes and forces players to carry the puck.

The number of touches of the puck allowed before passing changes the game. The principle is: the fewer touches the more important it is to anticipate the next play. Not only for the puck carrier but also for the potential pass receivers. Here are some touch rules:

1 One touch only before passing – The player must look before receiving a pass and offensive support must be immediate.

2 Two or more touches before passing – The more touches the more time the puck carrier has to make a decision, and teammates have to get open.

Specific skills are worked on by requiring the player to do tasks before passing. Some examples of these are:

1 Player can only pass when moving forward.

2 Player can only pass when moving backward.

3 Player can only pass while moving sideways.

4 Player must pivot in a circle before passing.

You can see that corrective games with modified rules are effective ways to use the game to teach players all of the physical and mental skills needed in hockey.

GAMES METHOD FOUR

- Play five-on-five either full ice or across the rink in one end. The players can be in the players box or lined up along the boards in the neutral zone.

- Break the five-player unit into units of three-on-three and two-on-two. This gives a continuous two-on-two and three-on-three game. The team of two can consist of two forwards, two defensemen or one forward and one defenseman. The teams of three can be created with three forwards, two forwards and one defenseman or two defenseman and one forward. They can play either following the 1-2-3-4-5 principles of reading and reacting or by assuming the role of a forward or defenseman. When the units of five play the "attack, defend, leave system" the game flows in this manner. Begin with a three-on-three game. When the defending team wins the puck, they break out of the zone and attack two defenders who are waiting just outside of the blueline. The three players go to the bench and are replaced by two teammates. The original defenders now attack in the other direction three-on-two. Two defenseman follow and wait in the neutral zone.

The flow of the game is as follows; 3-3, 3-2, 2-2, 2-3, 3-2, 3-3, 3-2, etc.

Another method is to divide the five players into three smaller groups of 2-2-1. This creates a flow which 2-2, 2-2, 2-2, 2-1, 1-1, 1-2 then repeat.

GAME TABLE

8 TEAMS	7 TEAMS	6 TEAMS	5 TEAMS	4 TEAMS
A-B	A-B	A-B	A-B	A-B
C-D	C-D	C-D	C-D	C-D
E-F	E-F	E-F		E
G-H	G			B-G
B-C	B-C	D-F	C-A	A-D
E-D	E-D	B-E	E-B	
G-F	G-F	A-C	D	A-D
A-H	A			B-D
D-A	D-A	E-A	E-A	
F-C	F-C	F-C	D-B	6 games
H-E	G-B	D-B	C	
G-B	E			
G-C	G-C	C-B	E-D	
A-E	E-A	F-A	B-C	
D-B	D-B	D-E	A	
H-F	F			
E-B	B-E	C-E	A-D	
C-H	F-D	D-A	E-C	
F-D	G-A	B-F	B	
G-A	C			
H-D	B-F	15 games	10 games	
A-C	E-G			
E-G	D			
C-E	C-E			
B-H	G-D			
G-D	F-A			
F-A	B			
28 games	21 games			

General Playing Principles

• Develop big moves separating the upper and lower halves of the body.

• The most important response when you get the puck is to drive-skate with it to open ice, taking 3 to 6 quick steps. This changes passing angles and gives you time to make plays.

• The best power skating drill is to scrape the ice, or do an activity that mimics scraping.

• Protect the puck with the body.

• Most North Americans hold their hands too far apart, eliminating the possibility of big moves, restricting the ability to move the puck creatively. This technique makes the bottom hand dominant and causes problems when taking and making passes. Hands should be held closer together and the top hand must be able to go across the front of the player, from side to side.

• Head and shoulder fakes should be encouraged

• Practice quick hands with the puck

• Quick feet.

• North American players are much too stiff, and only the best ones use big moves and fakes. This should be changed by allowing much more game play during practice.

• Europeans work on technique and mini games at early ages, doing skill circuits and tournaments in small areas with special rules.

• The four playing roles are a very good way to present the game and evaluate players.

SHARE *HOCKEY COACHING: THE ABCS OF INTERNATIONAL HOCKEY*

Order *Hockey Coaching: The ABCs of International Hockey* at $19.95 per book
plus $4.00 (total order) for shipping and handling.

Number of copies _____ x $19.95 = $ _____

Shipping and handling _____ = $ ___4.00___

In Canada add 7% GST _____(Subtotal x .07) = $ _____

Total enclosed _____ = $ _____

U.S and international orders payable in U.S. funds./Price is subject to change.

Name: _____

Street: _____

City: _____ Prov./State: _____

Country: _____ Postal Code/ZIP: _____

Please make cheque or money order payable to:

TM Sports Consultants   **FAX: 403-686-2419**
2435 – 38 Street S.W.   **E-Mail: tmolloy@cadvision.com**
Calgary, Alberta Canada T3E 3E6 OR: eha@utu.fi
                                   Internet Site: http://www.utu.fi/eha

For volume purchases, contact
TM Sports Consultants for volume rates.
Please allow 3-4 weeks for delivery.

SHARE *HOCKEY COACHING: THE ABCS OF INTERNATIONAL HOCKEY*

Order *Hockey Coaching: The ABCs of International Hockey* at $19.95 per book
plus $4.00 (total order) for shipping and handling.

Number of copies _____ x $19.95 = $ _____

Shipping and handling _____ = $ ___4.00___

In Canada add 7% GST _____(Subtotal x .07) = $ _____

Total enclosed _____ = $ _____

U.S and international orders payable in U.S. funds./Price is subject to change.

Name: _____

Street: _____

City: _____ Prov./State: _____

Country: _____ Postal Code/ZIP: _____

Please make cheque or money order payable to:

TM Sports Consultants   **FAX: 403-686-2419**
2435 – 38 Street S.W.   **E-Mail: tmolloy@cadvision.com**
Calgary, Alberta Canada T3E 3E6 OR: eha@utu.fi
                                   Internet Site: http://www.utu.fi/eha

For volume purchases, contact
TM Sports Consultants for volume rates.
Please allow 3-4 weeks for delivery.

USING THE PRACTICE CARDS TO PLAN A PRACTICE

- The practice cards for levels 0-1-2 are on the following pages. These cards can be removed by tearing them out along the perforated lines.
- Complete one level before starting the next.
- The practice cards are organized in a logical progression so use skating card two before card three.
- The game cards are also organized in a progression. When planning a practice have a ratio of at least fifty percent games and fifty percent skills. The games are designed to complement the skill modules and each game has a theme the coach should stress.
- It is a good idea to laminate the cards to make them more durable.
- Cards for levels 3-4-5-6 will be available in the 1998-1999 season.

We are available to give clinics to introduce the program. Ideally, hockey organizations looking for a world-class curriculum will implement this program throughout their system.

To get more information about clinics and seminars contact us using the information on the order forms.

Visit our internet site at http://www.utu.fi/eha
or
http://members.tripod.com/~Tom_Molloy/index.html

I Level 0 **SKATING**

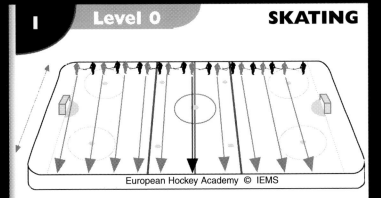

European Hockey Academy © IEMS

A1 BASIC FORMATION

Description:
The players are lined up along the side boards. The exercises are done with either one or two groups.

Teaching points:
A1 is the most basic of all the formations, and is the used first in the teaching system, because the skating distance is short.

Divide the players into small groups according to the colours of their jersey or simply number the players so that they have room to maneuver without colliding with another player. When the first group has reached the opposite boards, then the next group leaves. Repeat the same methods back the other way.

A1-0001

2 Level 0 **SKATING**

European Hockey Academy © EMS

0. A1, Module 2

- Walk on ice.
- Walk and glide on two skates.
- Walk and glide on two skates with knees bent over toes.
- Stationary jumps on two skate.
- Snowplough skate by toeing out and then toeing in with both skates at once.
- Snowplough stop by sitting low and pushing the inner skate edges into the ice.
- Run on ice and snow plough stop.
- Toe in toe out skate using the right skate to cut a "C" into the ice and the left leg to steer.
- Toe in toe out skate using the left skate to cut a "C" into the ice and the right leg to steer.
- Toe in toe out skate alternating feet, the sequence is stroke-glide, stroke with other skate, glide.
- Flat footed toe in toe out skate and then glide on one foot.
- T-push followed by glide.

A1-0003

2b · Level 0 · SKATING

European Hockey Academy © IEMS

0. A1, Module 3

- T-push start followed by glide.
- "Duck walk".
- Glide on one foot.
- Glide on one foot with the other knee held up.
- Push a partner down the ice from behind.
- Do 3-5 half squats while skating down the ice.
- Fast snow plow skating.

A1-0004

1b · Level 0 · SKATING

European Hockey Academy © IEMS

0. A1, Module 1

- Skating posture in forward skating. Knees bent over toes, back upright, head on top of shoulders.
- Stand on the inside edge of the skates.
- Stand on the outside edge of the skates.
- Stand on one skate.
- Stand on one skate and kick back and forth.
- Stand on one skate and kick side to side across the body.
- Push a chair or large pylon.
- Walk on ice.

A1-0002

3 **Level 0** **SKATING**

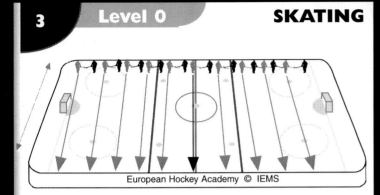

European Hockey Academy © IEMS

0. A1, Module 4

• Fast snow plough skating .
• "Slalom skating".
• Snow plough stop while skating forward. Start with the toes pointed in and then lower the seat while pushing out with the inside skate edges.
• Skate forward with both skates on ice, "flat footed skating"
• Follow the coach who skates slowly around the rink with knees bent and long strides.

A1-0005

4 **Level 0** **SKATING**

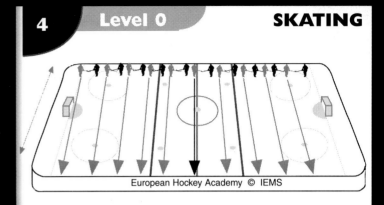

European Hockey Academy © IEMS

0. A1, Module 6

• Glide on one foot while the other knee is held up.
• T-push start with glide.
• Push a partner down the ice.
• "Flat footed skating" skating forward with both skates on ice.
• Glide on one skate.
• Glide on one skate with the other knee raised.
• Thrust and push with one skate while gliding on the other.
• Skate forward and do a one foot gliding stop by extending one skate in front and sitting low with knees bent and scraping the ice in front by turning the blade towards the middle so the inside edge is pushing against the ice.
• Skate backwards and do a one foot stop by extending one skate behind and sitting low with knees bent and scrape the ice behind by turning the blade towards the outside so the inside edge is pushing against the ice.

A1-0007

4b | Level 0 | **SKATING**

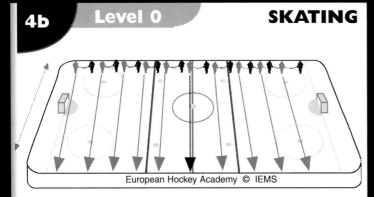

European Hockey Academy © IEMS

0. A1, Module 7

- Walk across the ice.
- While standing on the same spot, try and bend the body in all possible positions.
- Walk to a puck, bend over, pick up the puck, return to starting point and repeat.
- While standing try to stand on one foot, then the other.
- Walk and then glide on two feet.
- Take a puck in the hand and throw it ahead of you, go to it, pick it up and repeat the exercise until you have crossed the width of the rink.

A1-0008

by Gaston Schaeffer

The ABCs of International Hockey
Juhani Wahlsten – Tom Molloy

3b | Level 0 | **SKATING**

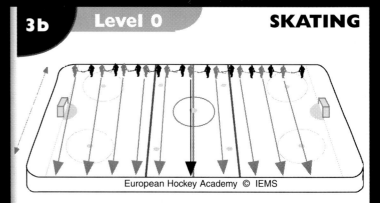

European Hockey Academy © IEMS

0. A1, Module 5

- "Backward skating posture"; seat down, back upright, knees bent, head on top of shoulders.
- Push off from the boards and glide with two skates.
- Half squats while gliding backwards.
- "Duck walk" with toes in.
- Swivel hips from side to side and slalom backwards across the ice.
- Backward snow plow stop. Sit low and push out with the inside edges of the skates.
- Skate backwards by sitting low and bending the knees past the toes, back up and head on top of shoulders. Make a C cut starting with the right toe facing in, now glide and do the same C cut using the left skate. Skate across the ice with the rhythm of: right stride-glide-left stride-glide.
- Pull a partner with one stick in each hand while skating backwards. Stress bent knees and toeing in then out using the inside edges of the blade.

A1-0006

5 Level 0 **SKATING**

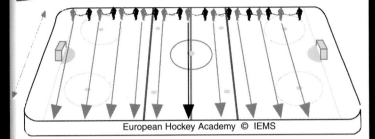

European Hockey Academy © IEMS

0. A1, Module 8

• Walk on ice.
• The coach spreads pucks all around on the other side of the ice. Walk to where the pucks are, by stepping over the sticks laid on the ice. See how many pucks you can collect.
• Put hurdles on the ice (60-70 cm in height) get the skaters to pass under it to go and collect the pucks. (this forces them to bend the knees).
• Combine the going over the sticks and under the hurdles, to provide a new challenge.
• Introduce the tennis ball. Start by passing the ball from one hand to the other while walking across the width of the arena.
-Try to do the same thing while skating backwards. (Short period of time to prevent boredom and frustration)

A1-0009

by Gaston Schaeffer

---

6 Level 0 **SKATING**

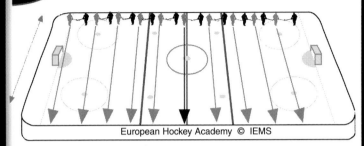

European Hockey Academy © IEMS

0. A1, Module 10

• Skate while passing the puck from one foot to the other.
• Skate while bouncing the ball from one hand to the other in the same time as you move from one foot to the other.
• Skate passing the ball from one hand to the other as you skate from one foot to the other.
• Skate passing the puck between the feet and the ball from hand to hand while skating forward.
• Same exercise as above but backward.
• Put some hurdles and try to jump over (10cm) and slide under others (40cm).
• To increase the level of difficulty, add low hurdles asking the skaters to first step over while bouncing the ball on the ice.
• Spread pucks around the ice and the players move around the ice and pick up the pucks by bending their knees and keeping a straight back. They then put the pucks into the puck bag. This activity works on the proper skating posture and balance. A1-0011

by Gaston Schaeffer

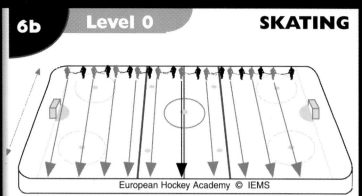

European Hockey Academy © IEMS

0. A1, Module 11

• Skate fwd and hop over a low hurdle then as quickly as possible turn around and catch the ball thrown by a team mate or a coaching assistant.
• Same as above but upon landing turn around the opposite direction.
• Skate fwd and hop over the hurdle, then fall and roll and get up immediately, turn around and catch the ball.
• Same exercise but the other direction (turning around the other way).
• Jump over a hurdle, crouch under the next one then do a slalom around five pylons on one foot then jump over the last hurdle and catch the ball as you jump.
• Repeat the same exercise but doing the slalom on the opposite foot.
• Skate fwd stop and as you stop, you will catch the ball thrown to you at the same time as the stop command.
• Skate backward and then at the command turn around as your the partner throws the ball for you to catch. • Same exercise but turn around the other way. A1-0012

by Gaston Schaeffer

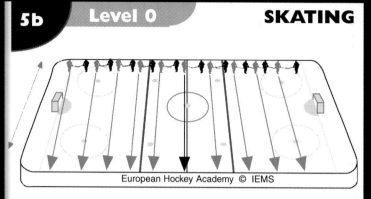

European Hockey Academy © IEMS

0. A1, Module 9

• Develop the glide by trying to pass the ball from one hand to the other as you stride..
• Introduce the bouncing of the ball while walking or gliding across the ice.
• Skate across the ice skating under and over hurdles of different height ranging from 70 cm -10cm.
• Skate backward by passing the ball from hand to hand.
• Skate backward by trying to move a puck between your feet .
• Skate forward by passing a puck between your feet.
• Skate forward passing the puck between the feet and the ball from one hand to the next.

A1-0010

by Gaston Schaeffer

7 Level 0

GAMES FOR BALANCE ON THE ICE

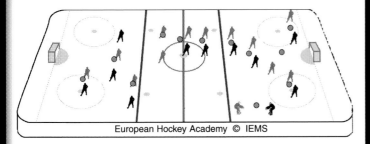

European Hockey Academy © IEMS

0. D, Role One

GAME OF CATCH WITH A PARTNER:

Play a game of catch with a partner. Use a ball and stand about 3-5 metres apart. This will stress balance on the skates.

D-0000

8 Level 0

GAMES TO DEVELOP ON ICE AGILITY

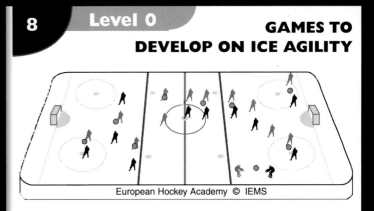

European Hockey Academy © IEMS

0. D, Role One

GAME OF KEEP AWAY USING A BALL:

The players must throw and catch a ball against another team. Play 1 ball for each 4 players (2 on each team), 2-2, 3-3, etc. Make sure all players have gloves to protect the hands from the skate blades. This game works all of the skating skills and develops split vision.

D-0002

8b Level 0

GAMES TO DEVELOP ON ICE AGILITY

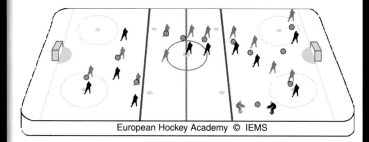

European Hockey Academy © IEMS

0. D, Role One

GAME OF HANDBALL ON ICE:

Two teams play full ice. Regular goals are used. All players must handle the ball before a goal counts. Use the ringuette crease, only the goalie can be in the crease. If the ball or Frisbee hits the ice the other team gets possession. All skating skills are practiced in this game.

D-0003

7b Level 0

GAMES FOR BALANCE ON THE ICE

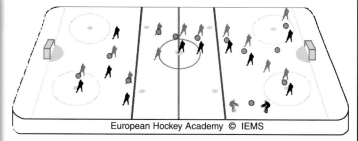

European Hockey Academy © IEMS

0. D, Role One

GAME OF CATCH WITH A PARTNER WHILE MOVING AROUND IN A SMALL AREA OF THE ICE:

Play a game of catch with a partner while moving around a small area of the ice, throwing and catching the ball. Groups larger than two can be used. This game helps in developing balance, using the edges, turning and stopping.

D-0001

9

Level 0

GAMES TO INTRODUCE GAME CONCEPTS AND CO-ORDINATION

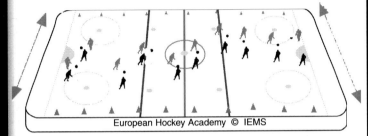

European Hockey Academy © IEMS

0. D, Role One

GAME USING ONLY THE FEET AS IN SOCCER FOOTBALL:

Each player has a pylon and places the pylons for goals all over the ice. The player dribbles the puck with her feet and scores at as many pylons as possible in one minute. The coach times the activity and has 5-7 games of one minute. After each game the coach asks who scored the most goals. Game skills are introduced and co-ordination on the ice is the focus.

D-0004

10

Level 0

GAMES THAT PRACTICE TEAM PLAY AND SKATING POSTURE

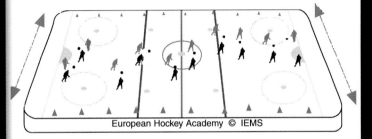

European Hockey Academy © IEMS

0. D, Roles One and Two

TWO ONE TWO GAME OF SOCCER FOOTBALL:

Play a cross ice game with the players in teams of 2. Score by kicking either the puck or a ball and hitting the pylon. One pass must be made. Offensive and defensive principles are learned, as well as change of pace skating.

D-0006

10b Level 0 GAMES THAT PRACTICE TEAM PLAY AND SKATING POSTURE

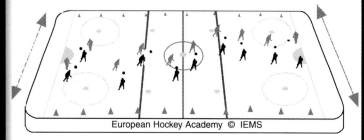

European Hockey Academy © IEMS

0. D, Role One

PYLON HOCKEY:

Use a large pylon instead of a stick. In this full ice game a goal is scored by pushing the puck over the other teams goal line with the pylon. This game practices keeping the knees bent and head up while skating.

D-0007

9b Level 0 GAMES TO INTRODUCE GAME CONCEPTS AND CO-ORDINATION

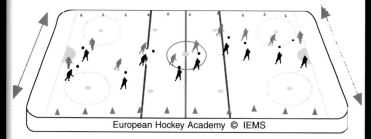

European Hockey Academy © IEMS

0. D, Role One

ONE ON ONE GAME OF SOCCER FOOTBALL:

The player scores by kicking the puck against the pylon. Each player has a pylon and places it across ice from his partner. Split vision, agility, and turns are emphasized in this activity.

D-0005

11 Level 0 GAMES FOR AGILITY, SPEED AND QUICKNESS

European Hockey Academy © IEMS

0. D, Roles One and Two

BRITISH BULLDOG:

This game has the players line up at the end of the rink in the A2 formation. One player is at the blueline and calls out British Bulldog. The players try to skate to the other end without being touched by the player at the blueline. If you are touched you join the player who is calling British Bulldog. To be good at this game the player must turn quickly, change speeds, and be agile.

D-0008

12 Level 0 GAMES FOR AGILITY ON SKATES AND BENDING THE KNEES

European Hockey Academy © IEMS

0. D

GAME OF FREEZE TAG:

Players play in one zone. One person is it. When a player is tagged they must stay in the spot they were touched. To be free another free player must slide on her stomach between the frozen players legs. This game uses all skating skills especially agility on skates. Make sure all players are wearing their hockey gloves.

D-0010

12b Level 0 — GAMES FOR AGILITY ON SKATES AND BENDING THE KNEES

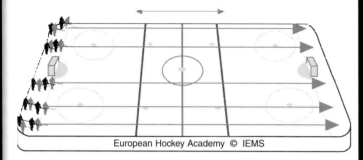

European Hockey Academy © IEMS

0. D

RACES PULLING A PARTNER WHO IS KNEELING

The players hold one stick in each hand and pull a partner one length of the ice. At the other end they turn and the partner pulls the first skater back. Stress bending knees and toeing out. This activity causes the skater to toe out, using more of the skate blade and a longer stride.
D-0011

11b Level 0 — GAMES FOR PUCK HANDLING AGILITY, SPEED AND QUICKNESS

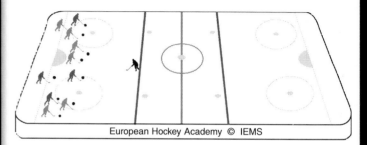

European Hockey Academy © IEMS

0. D, Roles One and Three

BRITISH PUCK DOG:

The players line up behind the goal line; when the player in the middle yells British Puckdog they stickhandle the puck, trying to get to the end, without being checked. If a player loses the puck they are in the middle checking. Last player with a puck wins.

D-0009

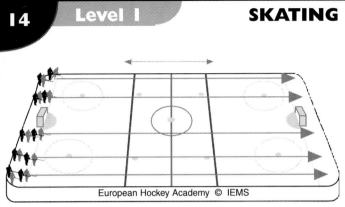

European Hockey Academy © IEMS

1. A2 BASIC FORMATION

The players are lined up at one end of the rink and divided into four groups. This allows the players to recover their energy between skating exercises and it also makes it easier for the coach to watch the players. Most of the exercises and tasks are done between the blue lines.

Organization:

The coach organizes the players into four groups. The first group leaves on the whistle. The next groups leave when the group ahead of them reaches the first blue line. The players stop at the end of the rink. These exercises are done lengthwise.

A2-1001

European Hockey Academy © IEMS

1. A2, Module 2

- Toe-in, toe out gliding between the bluelines.
- Group skating hold one knee up between the blue lines.
- Group skating and do squats between the bluelines.
- Group skating and do squats on the lines.
- Jump the lines while skating down the ice.
- Swing one leg forward and back as high as possible between the bluelines.
- "Shoot the duck" between the bluelines by squatting low on one leg while extending the other leg in forward.
- Deep squat and glide between the bluelines.

A2-1003

14b | **Level 1** | **SKATING**

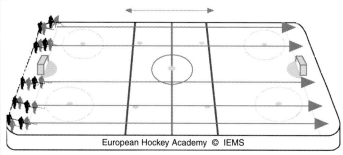

European Hockey Academy © IEMS

A2, Module 3

- Skate forward and hockey stop by sitting low with the knees bent, then extend the right leg forward and turn the foot in 90 degrees and start scrapping the ice. At the same time turn the right shoulder towards the skating direction and then the right hip. This causes the other skate to be parallel to the forward skate. Now scrape the ice with the outside edge of the trailing skate. Do this at each line.

- Do the hockey stop at each line and cross over start in the same direction by lifting the trailing skate over the lead skate and then pushing with the outside edge of the lead skate and striding using the inside edge of the other skate.

- Do the hockey stop at each line and use a running start by facing forward with the toes out and taking four to six quick strides. Stop at the next line.

A2-1004

13b | **Level 1** | **SKATING**

European Hockey Academy © IEMS

1. A2, Module 1

- Group skate from one end to another, using long strides.
- Group skating, holding one knee up between the blue lines.
- Group skating and doing squats between the bluelines.
- Group skating and doing deep squats on the lines
- Jump the lines while skating down the ice.
- Alternate front and back kicks between the bluelines.
- "Shoot the duck" between the bluelines by squatting low on one leg while extending the other leg in forward.
- Toe-in, toe-out skate and glide between the bluelines.

A2-1002

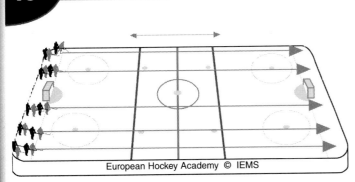

1. A2, Module 4

- Forward skating with extra long strides.
- Backward skating one length of the ice.
- Alternate front and back kicks between bluelines while skating backwards.
- Swivel hips while skating backwards with both feet on ice.
- Two backward figure eight's using toe out, toe in flat footed skating.
- Four backward figure eight's using toe out, toe in flat footed skating.
- Skate backwards and glide between the bluelines, emphasize good posture; knee's bent, seat down, with the head on top of shoulders and not hanging over the ice.
- Skate backwards and concentrate on toeing in and toeing out, cutting half circles with each stride. Weight should be over the middle of the skates.

A2-1005

1. A2, Module 6

- Face partner and push him down ice, stick at shoulder height.
- Toe-in toe out gliding between the bluelines.
- Snowplow skating slalom skating between the bluelines.
- Forward skating; with extra long strides. Knees bent, back slightly forward, head on top of shoulders.
- Flat footed skating, toe-in, toe-out. Stress bending knees and good posture.
- Two figure eight's while flatfooted skating. Stress turning the inside shoulder at the start of the turn. Push with the inside edge of the outside skate and glide with the outside edge of the inside skate.
- Four figure eight's while flatfooted skating. Stress turning the inside shoulder at the start of the turn. Push with the inside edge of the outside skate and glide with the outside edge of the inside skate.
- Skate forward and jump over the blueline and glide on one foot to other blueline.

A2-1007

16b Level 1 **SKATING**

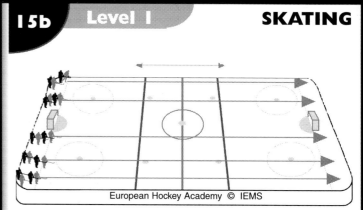

European Hockey Academy © IEMS

1. A2, Module 7

- Forward skate with extra long strides. Knees bent, back slightly forward, head on top of shoulders.
- Backward skate one length of the ice. Seat down, knees bent, head up and long strides.
- Backward skating one knee up between the bluelines.
- Backward skating with deep squats between bluelines.
- Backward skating with a deep squat at each line.
- Skate forward and make a high two footed jump over each line.

A2-1008

15b Level 1 **SKATING**

European Hockey Academy © IEMS

1. A2, Module 5

- Toe in and toe out skate and then glide between the bluelines.
- Skate forward with extra long strides.
- Skate forward and do multiple deep squats between the bluelines.
- Skate forward using flat footed toe in toe out skating.
- Two small figure eight's while flat footed skating. Stress turning the inside shoulder at the start of the turn. Push with the inside edge of the outside skate and glide with the outside edge of the inside skate.
- Four small figure eight's while flat footed skating. Stress turning the inside shoulder at the start of the turn. Push with the inside edge of the outside skate and glide with the outside edge of the inside skate.
- Skate one length of the ice backward. Seat down, knees bent, head up and long strides.
- Skate one length backward with deep squats between the bluelines.

A2-1006

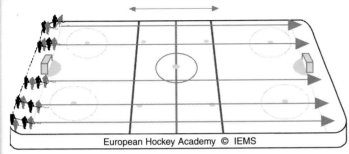

European Hockey Academy © IEMS

1. A2, Module 8

- Spread out around the ice and walk around a partner one way and then the other.
- Skate around the same partner by using cross overs. These are done by sitting low and turning the shoulder first. The outside leg steps over the inside leg and lands on the inside edge. The inside skate pushes under with the outside edge causing the skater to lean into the turn. Circle a partner one way and then the other.
- Return to the A2 position on the goal line and skate to the other end in groups. Turn a big circle in each zone, first one way and then the other. Keep the head up to avoid running in to other skaters.
- Skate forward doing a figure eight in the neutral zone.
- Skate forward doing a figure eight at each end of the ice.

A2-1009

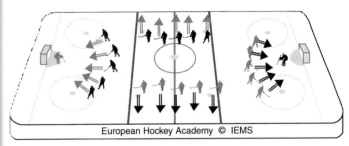

European Hockey Academy © IEMS

1. B1, BASIC FORMATION

This is the basic formation used in teaching shooting techniques. The players have pucks and line up within shooting distance from the board and the nets. The players will either shoot at the boards or the net.

Teaching points:

Practice a particular type for so many repetitions for example say, "practice 50 slap shots. The coaches should skate around so they can watch each player shoot and give the player feedback. Observe if the players are using the four phases of shooting. 1. Wind-up 2. weight transfer to produce force. 3. Release 4. follow through at the target. This is also a good time to watch the goalies basic stance and positioning.

B1-1000

18b Level I SHOOTING

European Hockey Academy © IEMS

I. B1, Module I

- Stationary shooting at the boards or net using the sweep shot
- Stationary shooting at target on boards using a back-hand shot.
- Stationary shooting at the boards or net using the wrist shot.

B1-1001

17b Level I SKATING

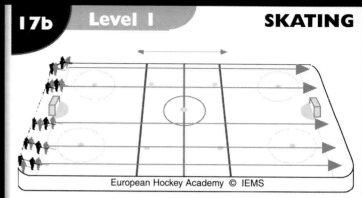

European Hockey Academy © IEMS

A2, Module 9

- Spread around the ice and walk around a partner backwards one way and then the other.
- Skate around the same partner. Glide on the outside skate with the weight on the inside edge. With the inside skate reach and plant the blade on the ice and then pull in using the outside edge. The outside skate stays on the ice and the inside skate does a series of PLANT AND PULL.
- Skate fast down the ice using back cross-overs. Start with the toes in and make a stride under to the inside with one skate, reach over this skate with the other skate and stride. Do three of these strides and then reach under to the inside with the other skate. These cross-overs are used for quick acceleration.
- Skate backwards down the ice using cross-overs for the first six strides and then making alternating C cuts with bent knees, back straight and seat down. Push using the middle of the skate blade.
- Skate backwards down the ice doing a figure eight in the neutral zone.
- Skate backwards down the ice with the stick held over the head in order to practice skating with the back and head up.
- Skate backwards the length of the ice doing a figure eight on each side of the red line. By doing this in a group it forces the player to keep her head up so she won't collide with another skater. A2-1010

GAMES PLAYED USING FULL ICE

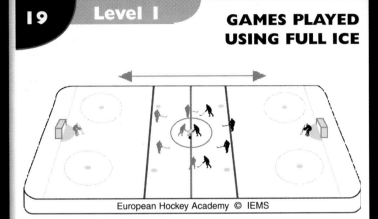

European Hockey Academy © IEMS

I. D1, BASIC FORMATION

D coded exercises are the most important part of the teaching system, because they involve the game itself. The other exercises all lead up to the D exercises as building blocks for learning how to play in game like situations.

Teaching points:

D1 uses the whole ice with two nets. The traditional and natural way of learning by playing using "scrimmages" is the model used, but rule variations enable the coach to use the ice more effectively.

D1-1000

GAMES PLAYED ACROSS THE ICE

European Hockey Academy © IEMS

I. D2, BASIC FORMATION

Games are played cross ice with nets, pylons, lines on boards, etc. as the goals. Special rules allow the players to practice individual or team play skills in this smaller area. In this formation many game understanding, reading and reacting skills will naturally be developed. This formation encourages creativity and split vision within realistic situations.

D2-1000

20b Level I — GAMES PLAYED ACROSS THE ICE

European Hockey Academy © IEMS

I. D200, EXERCISE

D200 formation is similar to D2 basic formation except the extra players line up along the blueline.

D200-1000

19b Level I — GAMES PLAYED USING FULL ICE

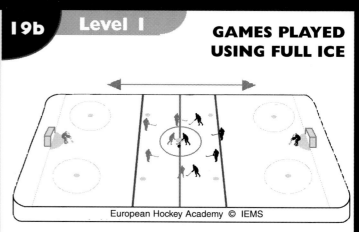

European Hockey Academy © IEMS

I. D100, EXERCISE

D100 formation is equal to D1 formation except the extra players are lined up along the boards in the neutral zone.

D100-1000

GAMES PLAYED ACROSS AND LENGTHWISE

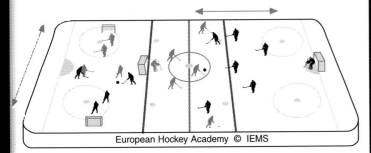

European Hockey Academy © IEMS

I. D3, BASIC FORMATION

In the D3 formation the ice surface is used by combining a full ice game in two zones and a cross ice game at the far end. This formation is very useful if the skill levels or size of the players vary. More advanced players can use D1, while the others play in D2 formation. This formation is very helpful when one end is needed to practice skills which don't have much movement. The game can go on in two zones, techniques can be taught in the other zone.

D3-1000

GAMES PLAYED USING ONE ZONE OR HALF THE ICE

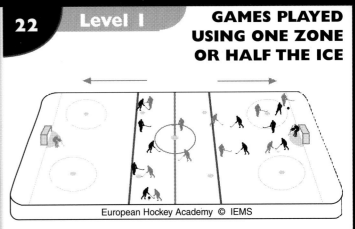

European Hockey Academy © IEMS

I. D4, BASIC FORMATION

In the D4 formation the players either use one third or one half of the rink and both teams shoot on the same net as in half court basketball. In order to go onto offence the defence must carry the puck over the blueline and then turn back into the zone. If half of the rink is available the defence must carry the puck as far as the red line before turning back and attacking. All players must get onside in these games, this rule promotes skating and much more realistic playing situations.

D4-1000

22b Level 1 — GAMES PLAYED USING ONE ZONE OR HALF THE ICE

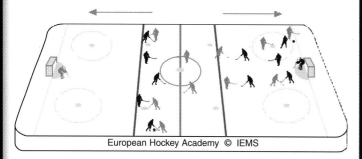

European Hockey Academy © IEMS

1. D400, EXERCISE

D400 formation is similar to D4 formation except the extra players line up along the boards in the neutral zone.

D400-1000

21b Level 1 — GAMES PLAYED ACROSS AND LENGTHWISE

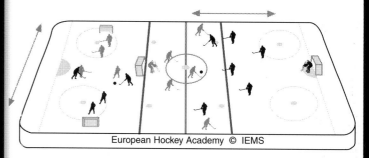

European Hockey Academy © IEMS

1. D300, EXERCISE

D300 formation is similar to D1 and D2 formations except the extra players are lined up either on the boards or the blue line.

D300-1000

GAMES PLAYED USING ALL THREE ZONES

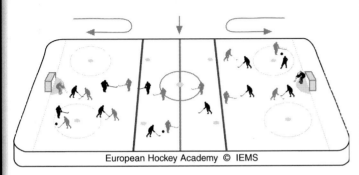

European Hockey Academy © IEMS

I. D5 FORMATION

D5 formation is the combination of D4 and D2. Two zones are used for playing half ice games where the players must touch the blueline with their skates before going on offence. The neutral zone is used for a cross ice game.

D5-1000

GAMES PLAYED WITH MANY PUCKS

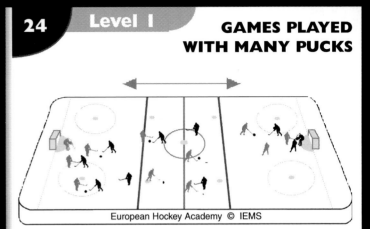

European Hockey Academy © IEMS

I. D1, Roles One and Three

PLAYING WITH MORE PUCKS USING FULL ICE

Playing with more pucks enables the coach to increase the amount of activity on the ice. More game like situations are created for the players to solve. To keep the game safe there can be no hitting or slap shots. All players should keep track of their goals. For beginners you can use many pucks and ask them to score as many goals as possible. After a while you ask how many goals each player scored, if the goalie is making a save the puck carrier must protect the puck and wait for the goalie to be ready before shooting.

D-1000

24b Level 1

GAMES PLAYED WITH MANY PUCKS

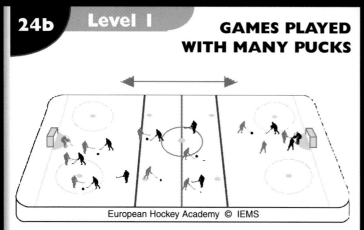

European Hockey Academy © IEMS

1. D1, Roles One and Three

PLAYING WITH 7 PUCKS

Two teams gather at centre and the coach drops 7 pucks if the goalie is making a save the puck carrier must wait for the goalie to be ready before shooting. The first team to score 4 goals wins, and another game begins. Make sure that there are only 7 pucks and the pucks are left in the net after a goal.

D-1001

23b Level 1

GAMES PLAYED USING ALL THREE ZONES

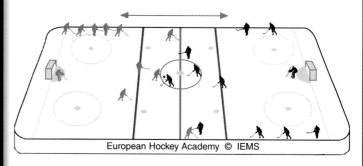

European Hockey Academy © IEMS

1. D500, EXERCISE

D500 FORMATION

D500 is similar to D5 except the extra players are lined up along the boards near the bluelines.

D500-1000

GAMES PLAYED USING TWO OR THREE PUCKS

European Hockey Academy © IEMS

I. DI, Roles One and Three

PLAYING WITH THREE PUCKS

Playing with 3 pucks causes some things to naturally happen. The players must look around with their heads on a swivel so they know what is happening behind them. Some methods are; everyone on the ice, 5-5 with line changes. Keep score and the team that scores twice wins. Next game start with two pucks, then one. In order to avoid confusion, only have three pucks on the ice at one time, the extra pucks can be on top of the nets. Another idea is a timed game where the goalie puts the puck back into play after a goal.

D-1002

COOL DOWN/ SHOOT-OUT

European Hockey Academy © IEMS

I. EI BASIC FORMATION

EI Exercises are meant to give the team a good way to finish the practice. The
formation is the same as B4 and CI.
I. Every player gets one shot at each net.
a. Score two goals, practice is over, hit the showers.
b. One goal, skate one lap, and go off the ice.
c. No goals, skate two laps.

Teaching points:

Team contests like a shootout, where players take penalty shots are fun for the shooters and the goalies.

EI-1000

26b Level 1 COOL DOWN/ SHOOT-OUT

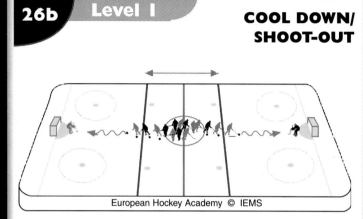

European Hockey Academy © IEMS

E1.05, 1-0

Players end practice by scoring in a shootout. They can leave the ice when they score on a breakaway from centre.

E1-1001

25b Level 1 GAMES PLAYED USING TWO PUCKS

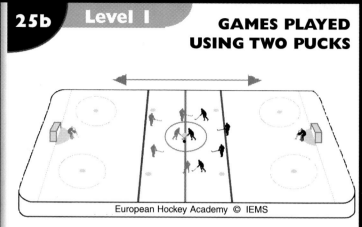

European Hockey Academy © IEMS

1. D, Roles One and Three

PLAYING WITH TWO PUCKS

Playing with 2 pucks has the same basic purpose in the system as all multi-puck games. The goalie puts the puck back into play after a goal. A good technique is to give a point to the team that scores two goals. Playing with two pucks at more advanced levels is a good read and react exercise when you play situations such as 3-3.

D-1003

European Hockey Academy © IEMS

2. A2, Module 10

- Toe-in toe-out scootering with gliding between the bluelines.
- Forward skating with extra long strides
- Jump over the blueline and glide to the other end on one skate
- Skate backwards one length of the ice.
- Hold one stick in each hand and pull partner down the ice backwards.
- Backward skate and raise stick above the head between the bluelines, this is to ensure the seat is down and head up.
- Skate backwards with extra long strides.
- Alternate forward and backward kicks between the bluelines while skating backwards.
- Two backward figure eight's.

A2-2000

European Hockey Academy © IEMS

2. A2, Module 12

- Toe-in, toe-out flat footed skating with a glide between the bluelines.
- Forward skating with extra long strides.
- "Zigzag" forward skating using crossovers.
- Alternate high cross kicks while skating forward.
- Backward skating one length of the ice.
- Skate backwards with extra long strides.
- Alternate high cross kicks while skating backwards.
- Backward crossover skating, stress keeping back upright, with head on top of shoulders, knees bent and seat down.

A2-2002

28b Level 2 SKATING

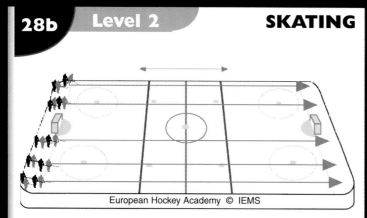

European Hockey Academy © IEMS

2. A2, Module 13

- "Zigzag" using crossovers while skating forward.
- Cross over while skating backwards, keep back upright, head over shoulders, knees bent and seat down.
- "Shoot the duck" one leg squat while forward skating between the blue lines. Squat low on one leg while extending the other leg forward.
- Start and stop on lines using toe out running start.
- Stop and start at lines while skating backwards, using a snowplow stop and cross over start.
- Start and stop on lines using the hockey stop and the crossover start.
- Backward starts and stops using the crossover start.
- Start and stop on lines using a running start.
- To practice stopping both ways have the players always stop while facing the same side of the rink.

A2-2003

27b Level 2 SKATING

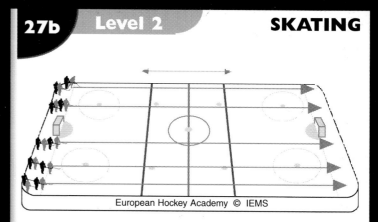

European Hockey Academy © IEMS

2. A2, Module 11

- Forward skating with extra long strides.
- Alternate cross kicks while skating forward.
- Two figure eight's with only outside skate pushing; lead with the inside shoulder.
- "Zigzag" forward skating, take three strides each way.
- Zigzag backward skating while pulling partner with one stick in each hand.
- Alternate high cross kicks while skating backwards.

A2-2001

European Hockey Academy © IEMS

2. A2, Module 14

- Standing jumps on two skates, 45-90-180-270-360 degrees.
- Using the A3 formation around the rink skate jumping on both skates from forward to backward and backward to forward at each line. Lead the turn with the shoulder.
- Using the A3 formation around the rink, skate gliding backward on one skate at the ends of the rink and doing a one foot turn to forward skating at the blue lines.
- Pivot from forward to backward and backward to forward at the bluelines.
- Skate along the boards and then down the lines pivoting from front to back and back to front at each corner.

A2-2004

European Hockey Academy © IEMS

2. A2, Module 16

- Forward crossovers "zigzag" skating.
- Two figure eight's with only the outside skate pushing, lead with the inside shoulder.
- Alternate high crossover kicks in forward skating.
- Crossover skating forward around the five circles with a maximum of six players per group.
- Alternate high crossover kicks while skating backwards.
- Two backward figure eight's.
- Skate backwards around the five circles.

A2-2006

30b — Level 2 — SKATING

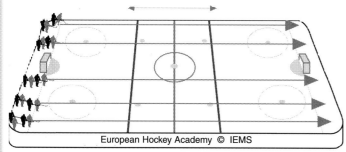

European Hockey Academy © IEMS

2. A2, Module 17

- Forward crossover skating zigzagging down ice.
- Two figure eight's while flatfooted skating "scootering".
- Four figure eight's while flatfooted skating.
- Crossover skating around five circles with a maximum of six players per group. Concentrate on leading with the inside shoulder and using the outside edge of the inside skate and the inside edge of the outside skate.
- Skate backwards around the five circles. Plant and pull with the inside skate.
- Pivot forward to backward and backward to forward around five circles. Keep the knees bent, seat down and lead with the shoulder and then open the inside hip and turn.

A2-2007

29b — Level 2 — SKATING

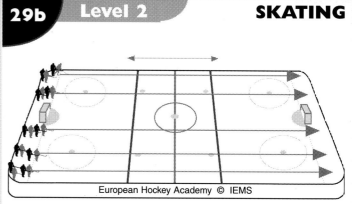

European Hockey Academy © IEMS

2. A2, Module 15

- Forward skating with extra long strides.
- Alternate high cross kicks while skating backwards.
- Forward skating with deep squats between the bluelines.
- Backward skating with deep squats between the bluelines.
- Alternate front to back kicks between the bluelines while skating forward.
- Alternate front to back high kicks between the bluelines while skating backward.
- "Shoot the duck" using a one leg forward squat and glide between the bluelines.
- Backward skating "shoot the duck" between the bluelines

A2-2005

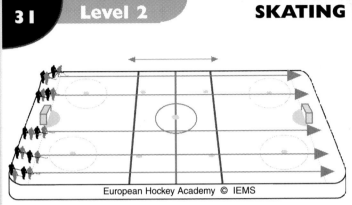

European Hockey Academy © IEMS

2. A2, Module 18

- Toe-in, toe-out flat footed skating gliding between bluelines.
- Forward skating using extra long strides.
- Starts and stops on lines using V or running start.
- Backward skating in a straight line.
- Alternate high cross kicks while skating backward.
- Skate full speed forward the length of the ice.
- Skate full speed backward the length of the ice.
- Start slowly from the end, speed up gradually and break to full speed at the blueline, glide in from the far blueline

A2-2008

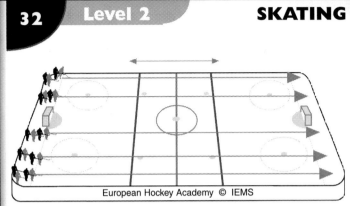

European Hockey Academy © IEMS

2. A2, Module 20

- Skate forward with extra long strides, stress bending the knees and seat down.
- Backward skating one length.
- Alternate touching one knee to the ice while skating forward.
- Drop on both knees at each line while skating forward.
- Alternate touching one knee to the ice while skating backward.
- Drop on both knees at each line while skating backward.

A2-2010

32b **Level 2** **SKATING**

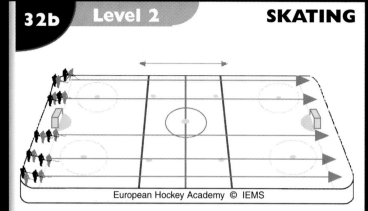

2. A2, Module 21

- "A2, 00 SKATING ROUTINE"
    - skate forward to the other end.
    - skate backward to the other end
    - crossover forward.
    - crossover backward.
    - pivot on the lines or on the whistle.
    - stops and starts on the lines or the coaches whistle.
    - tight turns on the lines or at the whistle.

A2-2011

31b **Level 2** **SKATING**

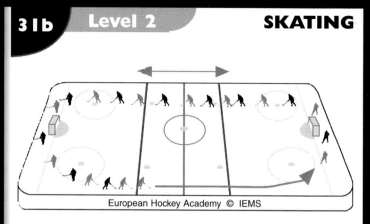

2. A2, Module 19

- Forward skating using extra long strides.
- Backward skating down the ice using long strides and bent knees.
- Start slowly from the end, speeding up gradually and break to full speed at the blueline, glide in from the far blueline.
- Using the A3 formation around the rink skate, gliding between the bluelines and skating hard at each end.
- Around the ring skate easy at the ends and hard between the bluelines.
- Skate backward gradually building to full speed by the far blueline.
- Skating backward starting slowly and breaking fast between the bluelines.
- Skate around the rink and start fast backwards using quick cross overs and coast between the bluelines and fast at each end of the rink.

A2-2009

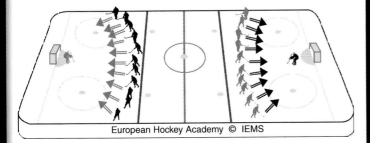

European Hockey Academy © IEMS

2. B2, BASIC FORMATION

Players are lined with pucks inside the blue lines. The distance from the net is determined by the age of the players and the type of shot being used. The harder the shot the farther from the net is the principle used.

Teaching points:

The simplest way is to start the shots from the left of the goalkeepers. In the middle of the exercise start from the right. You can have players; alternate from one end then the other, every second player shoot, skate in and shoot etc. Keep the shots below knee level and on the net. Players should focus on the netting behind the goalie and not on the goalie. Watch the goaltender to see if he centre's himself with the puck and if he plays his angles properly. The next player doesn't shoot until the goalkeeper has completed his save. If the players miss the net they must do some exercise such as push-ups etc.

B2-2000

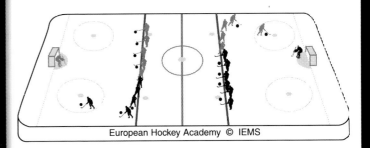

European Hockey Academy © IEMS

2. B2, Module 2

- Sweep shots while skating.
- Backhand sweep shot while skating.
- Forehand and backhand stationary wrist shot.
- Turn 90 degrees and make the row into a line. Take turns skating in and shooting from the end of the line.

B2-2002

34b Level 2 SHOOTING

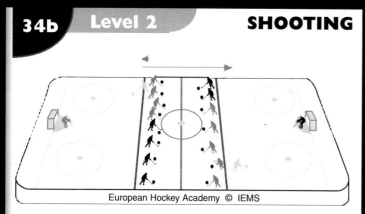

European Hockey Academy © IEMS

2. B2, Module 3

• Sweep shots while skating.
• Backhand sweep shot while skating.
• Forehand and backhand stationary wrist shot.
• Turn the row 180 degrees and face the opposite goal. Shoot on the far net skating one at a time through the players at the other blue line.

B2-2003

33b Level 2 SHOOTING

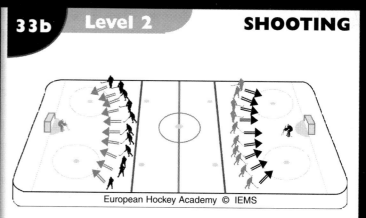

European Hockey Academy © IEMS

2. B2, Module 1

• Sweep shots in a line from various distances.
• Backhand sweep shots from different distances.
• Sweep shots while skating.

B2-2001

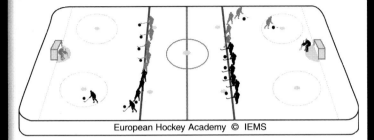

European Hockey Academy © IEMS

2. B200, EXERCISE

The basic B2 formation with the players in a row at the blue line. The players skate around the instructor or a pylon and take a shot on net. This exercise helps the goalie in playing angles.

Teaching points:

When cutting in the player should protect the puck with her body shielding it with an arm or leg. Move the pylon or coach in order to practice cutting in at various angles. Give the goalie time to prepare for the next shooter.

B200-2000

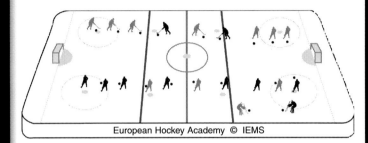

European Hockey Academy © IEMS

2. B3,1-0 BASIC FORMATION

The players line up in two lines down the middle of the ice. This formation is used to practice stickhandling and puck protection skills.

B3(1-0)-2000

36b **Level 2**

STICK HANDLINGATING

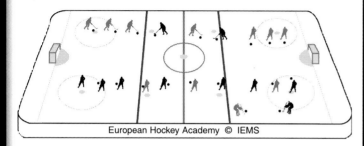

European Hockey Academy © IEMS

2. B3, 1-0, Module 1

- "Stickhandling techniques".
- Check the stick length to make sure the player can handle the puck across the front of her body and it is long enough to keep the head up.
- With no gloves grip the stick using only the top hand.
- Control the stick with both hands without gloves.
- Control the stick using only the top hand and roll the wrist.

B3(1-0)-2001

35b **Level 2**

SHOOTING

European Hockey Academy © IEMS

2. B200, Module 1

- Skate to the hash marks and take a sweepshot on goal.
- Skate to the hash marks and take a wrist shot on goal.
- Skate to the hash marks and take a backhand shot on goal.

B200-2001

37 Level 2   PUCK HANDLING

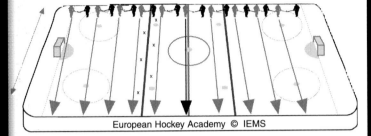

European Hockey Academy © IEMS

2. B3, 1-0, Module 2

- Stationary puck handling; move the puck narrow and wide in front and at each side of the body.
- Tight forehand turn with the top hand across the body and under the other arm. This helps the players separate the top and bottom half of their bodies.
- Place pylons about 4m. apart and .5m. on either side of the blue line, skate around the pylons and carry the puck over the line. The player must reach as far as possible to keep the puck on the line. This separates the movement of the top and bottom half of the body.

B3(1-0)-2002

38 Level 2   PUCK HANDLING

European Hockey Academy © IEMS

2. B3, 1-0, Module 7

- Have all of the players carry a puck in a small area, such as inside a face-off circle with about six players, or between the bluelines with a large group. The players weave in and out always protecting the puck with their body. On the whistle skate fast for about 5 seconds, then slow down on the next whistle. Various puck protection skills can be practised. Start with having them shield the puck with their body and whenever another player approaches, spread their legs wide apart and use head and shoulder fakes before swerving around the other player. Then have them hold the stick with only the top or bottom hand, this causes them to shield the puck, as they cannot stickhandle well with one hand.

B3(1-0)-2004

38b **Level 2**

PUCK HANDLING

European Hockey Academy © IEMS

2. B3, 1-0, Module 8

• Have all of the players carry a puck in a small area, such as inside a face-off circle with about six players, or between the bluelines with a large group. The players play keep-away always protecting the puck with their body and by using quick moves. On the whistle remove one or two pucks. Those players without a puck on the whistle must do a few push ups.

B3(1-0)-2005

37b **Level 2**

PUCK HANDLING

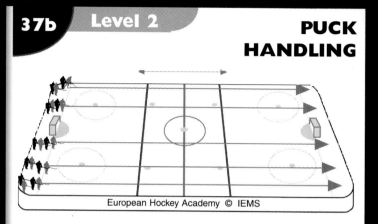

European Hockey Academy © IEMS

3. B3, Module 6

• Place a circuit of tires, pylons and small sawhorse type obstacles in four lanes up and down the rink. Make lanes from the boards to the offside dot, one down each side and one down the middle. The players leave from the A2 position behind the goal line in one corner, skate down the lanes, going through, over , under and around obstacles while carrying a puck. When they finish in the corner they skate behind the net to the back of the line. Move the line so that they are active 50% of the time. Shots can be incorporated in the circuit.

B3(1-0)-2003

PUCKHANDLING

European Hockey Academy © IEMS

2. A200, PUCKHANDLING ROUTINES

A200 formation is similar to A2 basic formation, except the exercises are executed with the puck

2. A200, Module 1

• Carrying the puck the length of the ice while skating forward
• Carrying the puck the length of the ice while skating backward
• Carrying the puck the length of the ice while zigzag skating forward
• Carrying the puck the length of the ice while zigzag skating backward

A200-2000

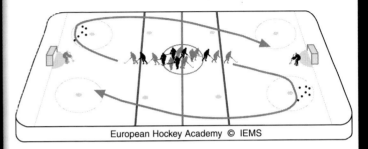

European Hockey Academy © IEMS

PUCKHANDLING ROUTINES

2. B4, Module 6

• Stickhandle the puck while skating forward
• Stickhandle the puck skating backward
• Stickhandle the puck, one figure eight between the blue lines while skating forward
• Stickhandle the puck, one figure eight between the blue lines while skating backward

B4-2000

40b Level 2

PUCKHANDLING

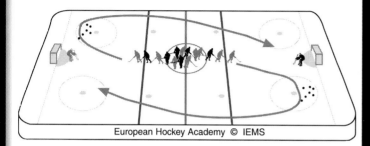

European Hockey Academy © IEMS

2. B4, Module 7

- Stickhandle the puck around the face off circles with forward cross overs.
- Stickhandle the puck around the face off circles while skating backward
- Stickhandle the puck with pivots on the lines. Alternate directions at each line

B4-2001

39b Level 2

PUCKHANDLING

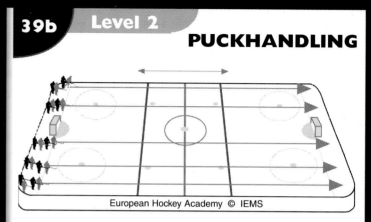

European Hockey Academy © IEMS

2. A200, Module 2

- Carrying the puck the length of the ice skating two figure eight's, one on each side of the red line while skating forward
- Carrying the puck the length of the ice while skating backward, making two figure eight's, one on each side of the red line.
- Carrying the puck the length of the ice while pivoting in a circle, to the right at one blue line and to the left at the other.

A200-2001

41 Level 2 PUCKHANDLING

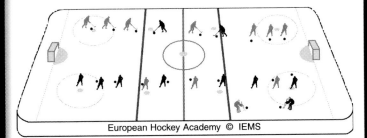

European Hockey Academy © IEMS

PUCKHANDLING ROUTINES TO SEPARATE THE UPPER AND LOWER PARTS OF THE BODY

2. B4, Module 8

- Stickhandle the puck, one figure eight between the blue lines while skating forward
- Stickhandle the puck, one figure eight between the blue lines while skating backward
- Stickhandle the puck, making two figure eights one on each side of the red line, while skating forward
- Stickhandle the puck, one figure eight on each side of the red line, while skating backward

B4-2002

42 Level 2 PASSING – RECEIVING

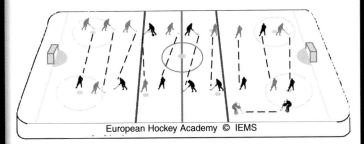

European Hockey Academy © IEMS

2. B3,2-0, FORMATION

The players line up facing each other parallel to boards. This formation allows them to learn passing skills. Teach the four phases of passing.

1. Wind up.
2. Force production by weight transfer from back to forward.
3. Release.
4. Follow through at the target.

Passes should be disguised within the stickhandling motion and wrist passes should be used. Listen that the puck isn't slapped and the pass receiver keeps her blade square to the puck and has soft hands to receive the pass.

B3(2-0)-2000

42b Level 2 — PASSING – RECEIVING

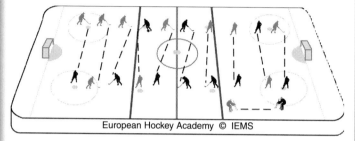

European Hockey Academy © IEMS

2. B3, 2-0, Module 1

- Keep the stick on the ice and square to the puck to take a pass. Keep the hands relaxed and give with the puck. The players should wrist pass by bringing the puck back for a wind up and rolling the wrists like they do when shooting a wrist shot. The passes should be quiet, no slapping noise or banging when they take the pass.
- Forehand passing with a partner.
- Backhand passing with a partner.
- Practice eye contact between the passer and the receiver by passing 3-4 pucks across to different players in the opposite line, make sure there is eye contact before passing.

B3(2-0)-2001

41b Level 2 — PUCKHANDLING

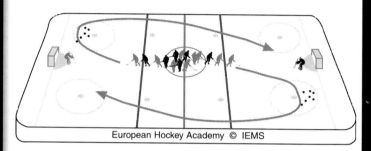

European Hockey Academy © IEMS

2. B4, Module 9

- Make a figure eight while carrying the puck on the forehand side of the stick while skating forward
- Make a figure eight while carrying the puck on the backhand side of the stick while skating backward
- Make two figure eight's while carrying the puck on the forehand side of the stick while skating forward
- Make two figure eight's while carrying the puck on the forehand side of the stick while skating backward

B4-2003

European Hockey Academy © IEMS

D, Orientation

PLAYING ROLES 1-3 IN PRACTICE

A cross ice game of 1 on 1 is the simplest and the best way to teach the role of the puck carrier (#1) and the checking player (#3) in practice. The player either attacks or defends during a 1 on 1 game and the transition from defence to offence and vice-versa is automatically experienced. The players are organised in pairs and play a cross ice game for one minute. When the game ends the players on one side of the ice move down one goal, with the last player moving to the empty goal at the other end. Play one game against each player on the other side of the rink; the players keep track of their wins, losses and ties.

D-2000

European Hockey Academy © IEMS

D, Orientation

THE AMOUNT OF PASSES AND LEARNING THE GAME

An effective way to teach the four playing roles is to have rules about how many passes are allowed. The less passes the more individual play (role #1 and role #3). The more passes the more team play (role #2 and #4).

D-2002

44b Level 2 GAMES TO LEARN THE FOUR PLAYING ROLES

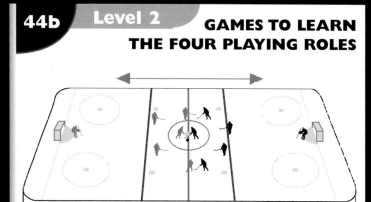

European Hockey Academy © IEMS

D, Orientation

CHANGING THE FOUR PLAYING ROLES WITH MORE THAN TWO PLAYERS

When the players understand the constant changing of playing roles in the 2 on 2 games they are ready for 3 on 3 and then 4 on 4 games. These games add the dimensions of the triangle and box in offensive and defensive situations. Play a cross ice game in each zone for two minutes and then have the teams on one side move down one goal and the last team go to the empty net at the other end of the rink.

D-2003

43b Level 2 GAMES USING SMALL TEAMS

European Hockey Academy © IEMS

D, Orientation

PLAYING ROLES 1-2-3-4 IN PRACTICE

5 cross ice games. The players experience the four playing roles in practice during a 2 on 2 game the players continuously change their playing roles from a puck carrier (#1) to offensive support (#2) or closest checker (#3) to the defensive support (#4). The players are organised in pairs and play a cross ice game for two minutes. When the game ends the players on one side of the ice move down one goal, with the players at one end moving to the empty goal at the other end. Play one game against each team on the other side of the rink; the players keep track of their wins, losses and ties.

D-2001

45 Level 2 — GAMES USING FULL ICE AND SMALL TEAMS

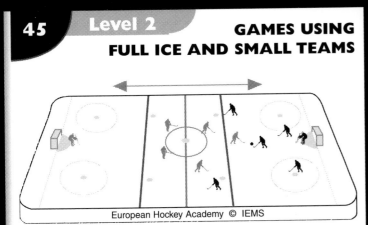

European Hockey Academy © IEMS

2. D, Orientation

FULL ICE SMALL AND MODIFIED GAMES

Play full ice micro games of 1-1, 2-2, 3-3 to practice the four playing roles in the defensive, neutral and offensive zones. Use modified rules to create the situations that you want the players to practice. These rules can be designed to practice good habits (always face the puck), develop skills (only wrist passes are allowed) or team play concepts (two points for a goal scored from a play originating below the goal line encourages offensive cycling and low defensive coverage).

D-2004

46 Level 2 — GAMES USING ONE ZONE AND OBSTACLE COURSES

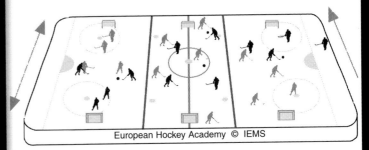

European Hockey Academy © IEMS

2. D, Orientation

GAMES AND EXTRA EQUIPMENT

Small nets, boards to divide the rink, old tires for targets, bars to jump over or skate under, balls and any obstacle are excellent aids to practice hockey skills. Create circuits that use this kind of equipment in order to practice skills.

D-2007

46b **Level 2**

GAMES TO PRACTICE GOOD HABITS

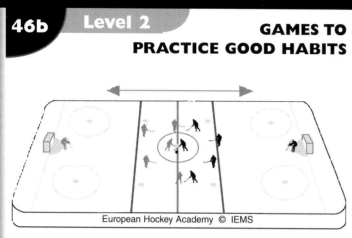

European Hockey Academy © IEMS

2. D, Roles One and Two

GAME STRESSING EYE ON THE PUCK \ GOOD POSTURE

A fundamental rule is that the players must always face the puck during a game. Everything that happens in hockey is relation to the puck and the players must see the puck in order to know their playing role and be able to switch from one role to the other. This helps eliminate unnecessary turns, and useless skating. At the same time the coach can emphasise the proper skating posture, so that players are always in the ready position.

D-2010

45b **Level 2**

GAMES USING ONE ZONE AND OBSTACLE COURSES

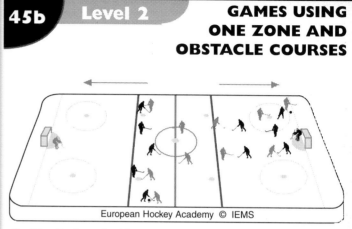

European Hockey Academy © IEMS

2. D, Orientation

A HALF ICE GAME WITH BOTH TEAMS SHOOTING ON ONE GOAL

Play a half ice game using any number of players. Individual skills can be isolated in a one on one game. All of the four roles are practiced in a two on two game. At the more advanced levels, defensive and offensive triangles are used in three on three games and a box offence and defence on a four on four game. Five on five has all of the team play components. All even and odd numbered situations like the power play or the six on five can be practised.

Some methods of transition from defence to offence are:
• All players must get on side and the puck carrier must touch the red line before attacking.
• All players must touch the puck before scoring.
• Pass to new players who are waiting in the neutral zone and the attack, either against the original attackers or new defenders.

D-2006

47 Level 2 — GAMES TO PRACTICE GOOD HABITS

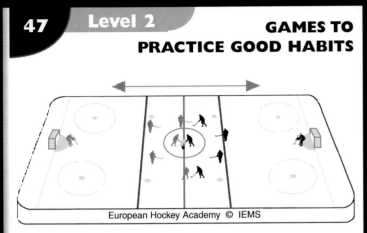

European Hockey Academy © IEMS

2. D, Role Two

FACE THE PUCK GAME:
Divide the players into teams of two or three. The rule is that the players must always face the puck during the game. This habit requires "hockey skating", which involves constant pivoting and turning to stay in contact with the play and enables the team to attack and defend as a unit.

D-2011

48 Level 2 — GAMES TO DEVELOP STICK HANDLING SKILL

European Hockey Academy © IEMS

2. D, Role One: Puck Protection Skill

GAME HOLDING THE STICK WITH ONLY THE TOP HAND AND PROTECTING THE PUCK:
The players are only allowed to hold the stick with one hand. This causes them to set up a wall to protect the puck with the body and skate to open ice away from pressure.

D-2013

The ABCs of International Hockey

Juhani Wahlsten – Tom Molloy

48b Level 2 — GAMES TO DEVELOP QUICK HANDS

European Hockey Academy © IEMS

2. D, Roles One and Three

KEEP AWAY:

Play keep away in one zone. Shoot a few pucks out of the zone every 15 seconds until only one puck is left.

D-2014

47b Level 2 — GAMES TO DEVELOP STICK HANDLING SKILL

European Hockey Academy © IEMS

2. D, Role One: Stickhandling Skill

GAME WITH HANDS CLOSE TOGETHER NEAR THE TOP OF THE STICK:

Play a half ice game, the rule is the hands must be close together at the top of the stick. This enables the puck carrier to make big moves and to roll the wrists and manipulate the puck more easily.

D-2012

GAMES TO DEVELOP QUICK HANDS

European Hockey Academy © IEMS

2. D, Role One

FAST HANDS

Everyone skates with a puck in one zone and weaves through the players using fakes and quick hands. On the whistle the players go full speed for 5-7 seconds and then go slower on the next whistle. Move the puck as quickly as possible during the speed bursts.

D-2015

GAMES TO DEVELOP A SOLID BASE AND QUICK MOVEMENT

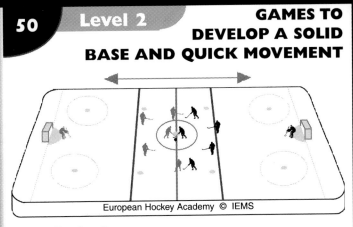

European Hockey Academy © IEMS

2. D, Role One

GAME WITH LEGS WIDE APART WHILE FAKING:

The player tries to combine the lessons learned in the other games. When he approaches the opponent he should have hands close together, legs wide apart, use head and shoulder fakes and protect the puck with the body. Pressure on the inside edge of one skate enables the player to turn very quickly.

D-2017

50b **Level 2**

GAMES TO DEVELOP STICKHANDLING AND BIG MOVES

European Hockey Academy © IEMS

2. D, Role One

GAME USING ONLY THE FOREHAND

Play a game by using only the forehand. The puck can be controlled only by using the forehand part of the stick. This game affects not only puck handling but also the movement of the players lower body. When the player changes the direction she has to skate around the puck and this opens up the hips and loosen the shoulder muscles. The wrists are used to pull the puck close to her skates in order to avoid being checked.

D-2018

49b **Level 2**

GAMES TO DEVELOP A SOLID BASE AND QUICK MOVEMENT

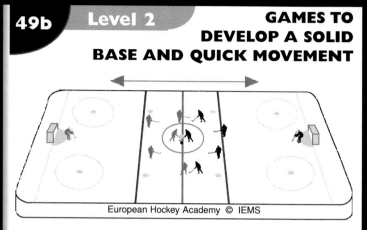

European Hockey Academy © IEMS

2. D, Role One

FLAT FOOTED SKATING:

Play cross ice or half ice allowing only flat footed toe-out, toe-in skating, where the blades never leave the ice. This is a good strengthening exercise as well as good practice in toeing in and out as well as unlocking the hips while skating.

D-2016

51 Level 2 GAMES TO DEVELOP STICKHANDLING AND BIG MOVES

European Hockey Academy © IEMS

2. D, Role One

"NO PASSING" GAME OF SHINNY WITH MANY PLAYERS

Play with large teams using "no passing" rule. The player with the puck must try to score by stick handling the puck through everyone. This game demands that the player practice the first playing role of the player with the puck and move her feet, pivot, fake, drive skate to open ice, etc.

D-2019

52 Level 2 GAMES THAT PRACTICE THE PLAYING ROLES IN ALL THREE ZONES

European Hockey Academy © IEMS

2. D, Roles 1-2-3-4

2-2, 3-3, FULL ICE GAMES

The best way of learning the four playing roles is to play 2 on 2 and 3 on 3 games. When playing these full ice games the normal rules, such as offsides, are enforced. These games with two or three players on a side make it easy to isolate the individual or team play skills that the coach wants to work on. The small groups keep all of the players actively involved and the coach can easily point out the techniques or tactics that are being done properly as well as those that need to be worked on. Organise by having the players line up along the boards in the neutral zone or sit in the players box. The shifts should be 30-40 seconds. Playing in small groups for 30 second shifts is a good way to practice support on offence and defence. Another option is to have the players change on their own when the puck is deep in the offensive zone.

D-2021

52b | **Level 2** | GAMES THAT PRACTICE OFFENSIVE SUPPORT AND INDIVIDUAL PLAY

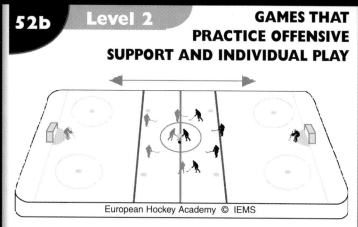

European Hockey Academy © IEMS

2. D, Roles One and Two

GAME WHERE THERE MUST BE AT LEAST ONE PASS BEFORE A GOAL COUNTS:

In order to practice roles one and two make the rule that there must be at least one pass before a goal counts. This rule encourages players to look for team mates and to get open for a pass.

D-2022

51b | **Level 2** | GAMES THAT PRACTICE THE PLAYING ROLES IN ALL THREE ZONES

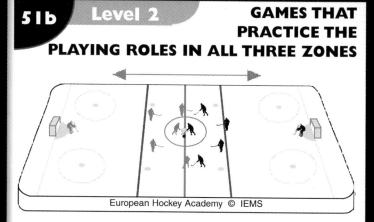

European Hockey Academy © IEMS

2. D, Roles 1-2-3-4

GAME STRESSING THE FOUR PLAYING ROLES:

Play a game and remind the players that they always have something to do during a shift. 1. Player with puck. 2. Offensive player without puck. 3. Defender covering puck carrier. 4. Defensive player covering pass receiver. When a "0" or loose puck situation occurs the player must realize whether they should think offence or defence first. Always protect against giving up odd man rushes and give the first player to the puck close support for passes and defensive help.

D-2020

European Hockey Academy © IEMS

2. D, Roles One and Two

GAME ALLOWING ONLY ONE PASS:

By allowing only one pass the player must try to score by drive skating to the net and team mates must support by screening, picking and going to the net for rebounds.

D-2023

European Hockey Academy © IEMS

2. D, Role One

QUICK HANDS AND FEET GAME

The development of the speed of the hands is often ignored when introducing hockey skills. When playing in tight, crowded areas, both quick hands and quick feet, moving at maximum speed are needed for the player to escape to open ice. When the hands and feet both move there is a separation of the upper and lower body motion and this makes the player difficult to defend. Play a full, cross or half ice game and emphasize quick hands and feet.

D-2025

54b — Level 2 — COOL DOWN/ GOAL TENDING SHOOT-OUT

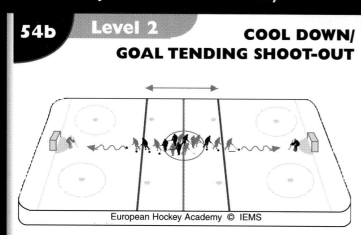

European Hockey Academy © IEMS

2. E1, CONTEST

Three options for a shoot out using two teams versus goalies, goalie versus goalie, etc.

1. One team versus the other team.

Each player gets one shot on each goal. The total goals for team are counted.

2. Two teams versus goalies.

All players shoot on each goal, saves vs. goals against are calculated.

3. Goalie versus goalie.

The same as #2 only the goalies compare how many saves they each make.

E1-2000

53b — Level 2 — GAMES THAT PRACTICE MOVING QUICKLY TO OPEN ICE AND FAST HANDS

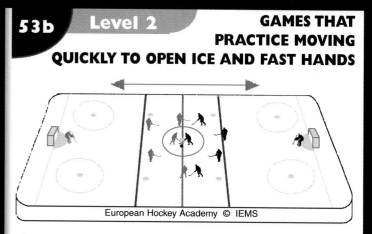

European Hockey Academy © IEMS

2. D, Role One

MOVING WITH THE PUCK GAME

Play a game with the rule that the players cannot pass the puck until they have taken 4 or 5 quick strides to open ice. By drive skating with the puck the player learns to find open ice and creates space for herself and opens up new passing lanes. Drive skating with the puck is fundamental for successful individual and team play and is one of the most important good habits to teach players.

D-2024

55 Level 2 — COOL DOWN/ GOAL TENDING SHOOT-OUT

European Hockey Academy © IEMS

2. G

G1, 01 • practice basic positioning; alignment, crease position, angles.

G1, 02 • work on lateral movement, angle alignment, telescoping.

G-2000

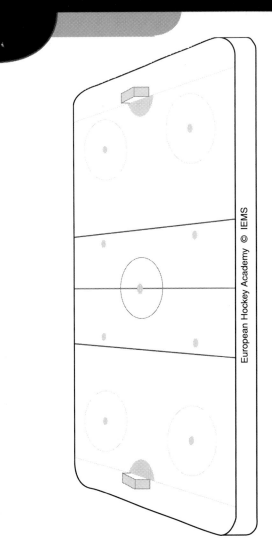

European Hockey Academy © IEMS

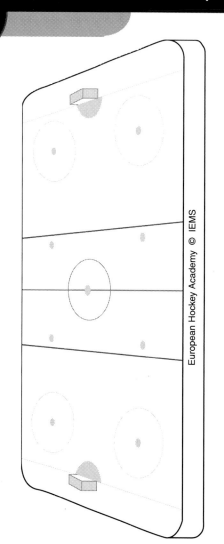

European Hockey Academy © IEMS

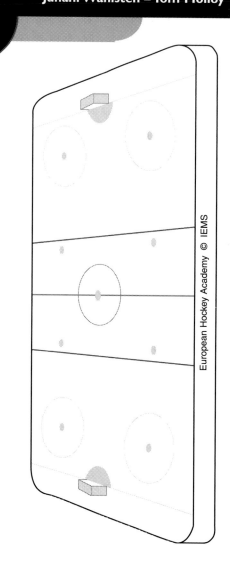

European Hockey Academy © IEMS